Mondays with my Daughter

Thoughts and meditations for moms and their girls

Heather Davis & Hadley Davis

Mondays With My Daughters

Italics or bold in Scripture indicate author emphasis.

Some names and places have been changed for clarity.

Interior Design by Road Trip Media, LLC
Published by Road Trip Media, LLC

Available in eBook publication and print publication.
Printed in the United States of America.

Cover Design: Lisa Kuehn
www.DreamonMarketingTeam.com

ISBN: **978-1546565871**

For the moms who have daughters ...
and for the daughters who have moms.

But especially for my own mom, Harriett Smith,
and my own daughters, Hadley & Briley

Introduction

When Hadley was about two, she "read" a book called *I Love You All Day Long*. The characters were these precious little piggies, one momma, and one child. The child pig doesn't want his momma to go work, leaving her little piggy in day care. The wise and strong momma tells her piglet she will love him all day long. When he's at the top of the slide, she will love him. When he gets into a squabble with a friend, she will love him. When he goes to the bathroom and avoids an accident, she will love him. And when she takes him home and tucks him into bed, she will love him. Throughout the book, the title phrase *I love you all day long* is repeated.

This was our constant "goodnight" book, and I, perhaps, related to the piglet more than the momma pig. It was a favorite of hers and of mine. So, it was really no surprise when Hadley, at the age of two said, "I'll read you the book tonight." And she did! It was, of course, memorized but precious nonetheless.

The next night, though, she said, "Momma! I wrote you a book!" She began to read the book she wrote which was exactly like the book *I Love You All Day Long*. She was two; she couldn't say copyright infringement or plagiarism much less know what they meant. But that moment, a writer was born.

At any given time, Hadley has a half dozen journals going; in some she jots down her thoughts with words, in others, pictures. She copies scriptures, quotes, and news happenings ... whatever is in her mind.

She is on the staff of the high school magazine and is in line to become editor as a junior next year. Already, she's a better writer than I am.

She came to me shortly after *Sundays At The Fields* was released and said, "I want to write a devotional with you," and I didn't think twice before starting this very book.

In this book, you'll read fifty-two devotionals, one for each Monday of the year. You can read them with your daughter, by yourself, straight through, or only on Mondays. We don't care how you read it; we just want you to enjoy it.

-1-

Sleeping Late

Many people were coming and going, so there was no time to eat. He said to the apostles, "Come by yourselves to a secluded place and rest for a while."
Mark 6:31

We've been out of school less than a week. During those seven days, we've taken three road trips, attended two parties (three if you count youth group), eaten exactly one meal at home, read two books amongst us, and watched uncountable hours of Netflix.

It's now 12:36 in the afternoon of day six of our summer vacation. Hadley is still asleep.

She's finished her first year of high school, has already begun thinking about her sophomore year, and has taken the opportunity on this lovely Tuesday to sleep.

Briley, however, has been up since ten. This is only because she really wants McKenna to come over to spend the night, and a clean room and bathroom are prerequisites for McKenna's arrival. Otherwise, Briley would sleep until much later in the afternoon.

I remember that season in my own particular life very well. I remember the days when I would sleep late and stay up later. I don't begrudge their late-sleeping ways. If anything, I'm feeling a little bit jealous.

The days of sleeping late would seemingly indicate there's not really a care in the world. No job to get up and work. No chores to get up and complete. No assignments to get up and finalize. No meals to cook. No clothes to wash. No dogs to feed.

Yeah ... I'm a little bit jealous.

But, if I'm being completely honest, I wouldn't go back to those days of being a teenager again. Sure, my abs were still tangible and my hair contained exactly zero gray, but the confidence I have now and the clarity with which I can see my future (or at least glimpses of it) are worth so much more than a bottle of hair color and a flat stomach (but barely).

The teenage years are indeed times when many people are coming and going, just as described in Mark after feeding the masses. Read all of Mark 6. ☺

We have first loves, mentors, neighbors, teachers, professors, best friends, frienemies, bullies, acquaintances, youth pastors, and even parents. They'll move seamlessly from our lives due to decisions, transfers ... all of them some sort of change. Each of them taking a part of us with them and leaving a part of themselves with us.

After the apostles had fed the five thousand, I can only imagine their fatigue. I feed my family of four on a quasi-regular basis and end up exhausted. I've yet to perfect the meal that will satisfy each of them at the same time. And no matter how many times I tell them to clean up after themselves, there's still ketchup stuck to a plate and chicken morsels pasted to the floor under the dining room table.

Jesus recognized the apostles' servitude and told them to find a quiet spot and rest.

Jesus recognizes a teenager's brewing storm called life and calls them to rest as well.

He recognizes my exhaustion and calls me to rest.

Oddly enough, the teenagers are the only ones wise enough to rest until the weariness is gone—waking at noon ready to conquer the world.

Heavenly Father, let me find my secluded place with You. Let me learn to rest away from the world knowing that You will provide me with everything I need to conquer the world in Your name when I wake. In the name of Jesus, who feeds me still today, Amen.

-2-

Panic In The Parlor

by Hadley

Throw all your anxiety onto him, because he cares about you.
I Peter 5:7

Being a part of our United Methodist church, I feel very loved and accepted, but it has always been hard for me to open up about my anxiety. Every Wednesday we have small groups within our youth group, and I am part of the high school girls. I couldn't love them more.

We spoke about trust on Wednesday night and our youth leaders split us up into pairs. I was lucky enough to be with one of my best friends. I was blindfolded and told to follow the directions she gave. We eventually ended up in our parlor, although I didn't know that at the time. The whole purpose behind the activity was to help us realize God guides us even though we can't see Him—we just have to listen.

Although I have struggle with anxiety, I like to appear more confident than I really am. I put on a mask of humor and confidence that I don't often take down. The faith walk truly brought my anxiety to the surface; I didn't like having one of my senses completely stripped away nor having to rely on a weaker sense, but I didn't let that show. Also, as much as I love my friend, I didn't like for her to be in control of me.

I laughed and joked through the whole thing until we got to our parlor.

We took off the blindfolds and waited for all of the groups to rejoin us. In that moment, I couldn't breathe. Tears gathered in my eyes, and I couldn't draw in complete breaths.

I was letting my mask down. I didn't want others to see, so I left the parlor.

I let the tears fall in the hallway. I did my best to catch my breath.

One of our leaders, an amazing woman named Jessica, checked on me. She hugged me; she guided me through breathing exercises; she told me how proud she was of me; she let me cry, judgment free. She gave me time to calm down and didn't rush me; she told me to tell her next time something didn't feel right; she would sit it out with me. She accepted me, flaws and all. When the time was right, we went back to the parlor where I got nothing but unwavering support.

Despite my panic attack, I learned a lot that evening. I learned that my youth group loves unconditionally. I learned to trust in God and all the amazing people He puts in your life. I learned that God works in ways not always known at the time.

How could I have known that I would be in that place with those friends when I suffered my first panic attack?

God loves me no matter what, and if he has put a person in our lives, they are meant to act as His hands, His feet, and His heart, granting us mercy and grace that can only come from Him.

Father in Heaven, You know us so very well that You have not only given us grace and mercy, but You've given us people who can deliver these things to us. Thank You for friends who will lead us and trust us as well as for leaders who step away from life—even if just for a moment—to give us a peace that comes from You. In the name of Jesus Christ our Lord I pray, Amen.

-3-
Endless Amounts of Sun-In

Instead, make ourselves beautiful on the inside, in your hearts, with the enduring quality of a gentle, peaceful spirit. This type of beauty is very precious in God's eyes.
I Peter 3:4

When I was Hadley's age, my neighbor had me babysit all night long so she could go to a twenty-four-hour dancing event at Disco International. She paid me $10 plus all the pizza rolls I wanted to eat after her boys went to sleep. The next day, once she was home and asleep on the couch, I begged my mom to drive me to the store where I purchased a bottle of Sun-In.

Once my mom was asleep on the couch (she hadn't been disco dancing, she just had teenage daughters), I locked myself in the bathroom with a spray bottle of water, a hair dryer and my bottle of Sun-In. I emerged almost three hours later with neon orange hair.

Sounds as hideous as Jake the State Farm guy, I know, but in 1984 it was glorious.

My dad, who had almost neon-orange hair naturally took one look at me and said, "What the $*#&" before retreating to the garage where he stayed until I turned 19.

And that was the start of my hair-coloring career. In college, I used to perm and frost other girls' hair in order to earn enough money to have my hair professionally done. Once out on my own, I would pay significant amounts of money to have my hair professionally colored because I was a premature gray-er. Eventually I became a mom and decided to go back to being a DIY colorist because of such things as braces and college.

A little over a year ago, though, the gray began to win at about the same time my girls began to beg. And really, it was only one girl: Briley. She wanted pink hair. No! Purple hair! Wait ... blonde highlights. Yeah! That's what she wanted. Any of it.

I stopped coloring my hair to not only teach her a lesson about loving yourself the way you are, but because I had visions of the gazillion dollars I was going to have to spend to fix her hair when she locked herself the in the bathroom after a lucrative night of babysitting.

The trouble with Briley was the same trouble I had as well: We have sisters with gorgeous hair. Growing up, my sister had beautiful, long, silky blonde hair. Briley's sister has wavy, thick, deep auburn hair. (Her hair was what I was going for when I first spritzed on the Sun-In. Very funny, God.)

It's a really hard battle to fight, trying to convince our girls they are beautiful. When God picked Briley and Hadley to be our daughters, he knew just how beautiful they would be. He knew that Hadley's hair would be auburn and that Briley's would be deep brown. He knew Hadley's eyes would be hazel until they turned brown and stayed that way. He knew they'd both be tall, tall, tall and that Briley would tan with ease, while Hadley's skin would be porcelain or red with no in between.

He also knew that they'd each have a heart with a capacity for love and forgiveness and openness and peace, but that each girl would have to decide on her own how that beauty would come through.

The world shows us through the Internet and magazines and television and movies what beauty looks like. God, however, shows us that regardless of our hair color, it's our behavior and our capacity for love that makes us a precious child of His.

Beautiful Savior, when we see the outside, remind us gently that You've already made us beautiful and given us a heart that can spread the wonder and loveliness of You. Give us eyes to see ourselves the way You see us so that through our actions, we can glory You. In Your precious name we pray, Amen.

-4-
It's Not Fair

As you know, we never used flattery, and God is our witness that we didn't have greedy motives. We didn't ask for special treatment from people—not from you or from others—although we could have thrown our weight around as Christ's apostles. Instead we were gentle with you like a nursing mother caring for her own children.

I Thessalonians 2:5-7

As soon as children learn to speak, they have a set battle cry: It's not fair!

"Can I have a cookie?" *Not now.* "That's not fair!"

"Can I stay up late?" *No.* "It's not fair!"

"She got to go with her friends. That's not fair!"

"But I don't like broccoli. It's not fair to make me take a bite!"

When our kiddos are little, we can explain that they can't have a cookie because it's almost dinner or they can't go to their friends because they are going to Grandma's instead or they have to try broccoli because it's healthy. For the most part, they'll accept our explanation without much fuss (depending on the day, of course).

But, soon enough, as their brains develop, their thought processes mature, and it becomes more and more difficult for them to take us at our word. They want more than just a one-word or one-sentence explanation. And, they become impassioned about their battle.

"I do not need sleep, Momma," a very young Hadley would say while yawning. I could convince her otherwise by lying in bed with her and speaking softly.

This is a stark contrast from a teenage Hadley who screeches at me from her desk as the midnight hour approaches while still working on a homework assignment. "Mom! Geez! I'll sleep when I get this finished. Back off, okay? I'll turn out my own light!"

The next morning, she's usually groggy, certainly crabby and, at some point, she most assuredly says, "This isn't fair." Typically, she's referring to her lack of sleep, the assignment, the fact that I made her get up and go to school as "the thing" that isn't fair.

It hurts to stand at my kiddo's doors and watch her make these stressful decisions. It was so much easier to tell her no cookie with promises of a soon-to-come dinner of chicken nuggets or macaroni and cheese. I know that my girl needs sleep. But she knows that she needs to finish her biology research paper. It's difficult for me to not rush into her room, send her to bed and write the paper myself.

But, that would serve no useful purpose at all.

Often times, we find ourselves in similar situations with our Heavenly Father. I'm sure I haven't stood in my bedroom yelling for Him to get back and let me handle things myself. But I know for a fact, there are many times I've ignored His guidance and done what I wanted to do. And, like my sweet, stubborn child, I find myself with my head in my hands, feeling groggy, cranky and crabby with cries of "It's not fair."

I often fight the urge (sometimes not successfully) to tell my kiddo, "I told you so."

God is a much gentler parent than I am. He doesn't entertain the notion of throwing my poor decisions in my face. He pulls me closer during my cries of "It's not fair," but gives me no special treatment or exemption from the consequences of my decisions.

His gentleness is evident after our steepest falls, our most agonizing moments and our most sleepless nights. If we learn to listen closer, we'll hear him softly guiding our decisions, but the rest is up to us—fair or not.

Father, many nights You stand in our doorways and encourage us to rest. You know that the unfairness of situations comes from our own decisions, yet You let us choose for ourselves. Thank You for allowing us to make the decisions we want and for waiting gently with open arms when we are crushed under the weight. Help us to listen more for Your voice and choose less based on our own desires. In Your holy name I pray, Amen.

-5-

We're Talking About You

Therefore, you should treat people in the same way that you want people to treat you; this is the Law and the Prophets.
Matthew 7:12

Our girls are twenty-six months apart. When our second daughter was born, I used to hold her in one arm, her older sister in the other arm, and dream of the day they would be best friends.

Now, I hold one at the end of one arm and the other at the end of my other arm, keeping them separate, wondering if they will ever be on friendly terms. Forget best friends, I'd just settle for them to not scratch, pinch, or punch each other for longer than a two-hour stretch.

While scripture is normally pretty good about setting up context for each passage, I'm thinking that maybe in some translation the Golden Rule was set up as Jesus talking to feuding siblings.

The girls were actually tweens when I first quoted the scripture from Matthew to them.

"I am!" Briley screamed back at me.

“You are treating her how you want to be treated?” I asked.

“I’m treating her how she’s treating me ...”

So close ...

As they continued to bicker through the years over such things as the color of Briley’s fingernails or who failed to flush the toilet (Hadley swears it wasn’t her), I’d try more and more to get them to see the relevance of what Jesus was saying.

This scripture is not about how we’re being treated. It’s about our own behavior, plain and simple.

Time and again, Jesus tells us to turn the other cheek, to not be guided by the ways of the world, to love others ... to treat others how we ourselves want to be treated.

“So,” I began during a momentary truce, “how do you want your sister to treat you?”

The usual words cropped up: Kind, Caring, Respectful, Nice, and Loving.

“When was the last time you showed your sister how to treat you?”

It was a loaded question, and no one likes to confess her sins before anyone, much less her own sister. The answers were not quite honest.

“I try all the time, but she ...”

“I do that, but she ...”

“But if I do that, she’ll ...”

Funny thing about the Golden Rule: Nowhere in any translation is the word **but**. Just a very simple command: *Treat others how you want to be treated.*

I know for a fact it's easier for my girls to live out this edict with almost everyone else but their sister. I know, I have a sister myself. It's so easy to play dirty with our sisters and brothers especially when they know exactly how to push our buttons and make us crazy without seeming to try.

How beautiful would the world be, though, if we could live The Golden Rule at all times with all people? Even our stinkin' sisters.

Jesus, You make it look so easy to turn the other cheek and treat even the nastiest of people with respect. Help us to be more like You in our words, our deeds and our behavior. Call us to a higher standard, even when dealing with our brothers and sisters. In Your peaceful and perfect name we pray, Amen.

-6-

All Natural

You've taught me since my youth, God, and I'm still proclaiming your wondrous deeds! So even in my old age with gray hair, don't abandon me, God! Not until I tell generations about your mighty arm, tell all who are yet to come about your strength, and about your ultimate righteousness, God, because you have done awesome things! Who can compare to you, God?
Psalm 71: 17-19

Two years ago, I chopped my hair off to a cute pixie and stopped coloring it. My gray had become resistant to doing anything I wanted it to do, and who really has the time and energy to keep up a color job?

My husband loved it. It was new to him. After almost nineteen years together, he'd never seen my original color except for the extra long month when my roots grew out between touch-ups.

A friend said it was "the most flattering cut" she'd ever seen and asked for my stylists' name and number.

My neighbor said she wished she had the guts to cut her hair and flaunt her natural color, but she wasn't sure what it would look like and wasn't willing to take the chance. But, she loved it on me.

My daughters? They begged me to color it! Grow it! Wear a hat! Do something! They weren't convinced it was a good look for me.

Briley, my younger daughter, was the most vocal about my gray. I am an "older" mom—I was 33 when Briley was born. I get where she's coming from. My mom was an older mom; I was embarrassed by her prematurely gray hair as well. She always had short hair. I would probably have thought it was weird if she'd have grown it out.

My older daughter, Hadley, thought I never should have messed with it in the first place. She let me know this in no uncertain terms.

"Like not cut it? Color it? What?" I asked.

"No," she replied, twirling a piece of her naturally wavy auburn hair, "you should have never colored in the first place when you were like a teenager or whatever."

I nodded my head. She had a point.

If I'd had her gorgeous locks on top of my head, I never would have touched them. Or whatever.

Hindsight is, of course, 20 / 20.

If I'd left the Sun-In alone ...

If I'd never touched my hair with a 400 degree curling iron daily for four years of college ...

If I'd only known then what I know now.

From the moment we are born, God is holding us, teaching us, breathing life into us. Somewhere along life's journey, we fail to recognize the knowledge He is giving us. Instead we make our own decisions. In my case, it was treating my hair poorly (amongst a host of other things I could share, but I won't because I have a word limit).

At the age of fourty-six, with gray hair and a stronger foothold on solid ground, I can look back and see that all along the way, God's been guiding me. And, through the grace that is forgiveness, He lets us right ourselves again and again and again.

My hair's increasingly gray, something I've embraced and now love. One day, my daughters will have their own gray hair (or another source of contention between them and their own children) and will understand the mercy our Heavenly Father extends to us and always will.

Lord and Father, Thank You for your guidance and for never failing to be ever-present even when we choose to do our own thing and choose to ignore the beauty You have waiting for us. Your grace is worth so much more than we can find on our own in this world. Your patience with us is a precious gift—forgive us when we go down a different path. Thank You that You continue to lead us, Lord. In the beautiful name of Christ we pray. Amen.

-7-

Play It Again, Sam

Whatever has happened—that's what will happen again; Whatever has occurred—that's what will occur again.There's nothing new under the sun. People may say about something: "Loot at this! It's new!" But it was already around for ages before us.
Ecclesiastes 1: 9-10

Disclaimer: Don't judge me based on our iTunes account. If anything, it's proof that God can take any of us and give us good words.

On the occasion of Prince's death, Hadley asked if we could download some of his music. I excitedly told her I already had it downloaded. I didn't tell her that I'd had it for quite some time. She thanked me and retreated to her room to, I assume, party like it's 1999.

A few weeks later, she asked me to download a little song called "We Don't Have To Take Our Clothes Off". Without any hesitation, I downloaded Jermaine Stewart's song from my college days and blared it through the speakers.

"No, Momma," Hadley sighed. She probably rolled her eyes as well. I don't know for sure because I was too busy dancing. "This isn't the right song."

How many songs can there be called, "We Don't Have To Take Our Clothes Off"? Well, friends, there are at least two. The version she wanted was a way toned down, piano-acoustic mix by Ella Eyre. (Who knew? No really, who knew? I had no idea.) I couldn't dance to Ella's version, no offense to Ms. Eyre, and wasted no time in telling Hadley this.

She wasted no time in telling me that it came closer to real music than Jermaine Stewart's version.

Agree to disagree.

[Agree to disagree: The sanity saving terms that most teenagers and their parents take over the subject of music, clothing, movies, pop culture and a good time.]

I'm confident that when she has kids of her own, she'll try, in vain, to get them to listen to Twenty-One Pilots and be heart-broken when they tell her that P!nk wasn't a great artist.

Some day in her future, a new, young artist will redo her favorite song twenty years from twenty-years ago, and she might take to her bedroom, close the door, and listen to the great hits of her time, while waxing poetic over the good ol' days.

It's a song as old as rhyme.

But, if I'm being honest, I've come to love the new and improved "We Don't Have To Take Our Clothes Off", and I'm a little bit terrified that she might take Prince's songs as gospel.

In our lifetime, we see many things that are new and improved. We hear different takes on the same ol' same ol' and debate the merits of the way things used to be versus the way things are progressing.

I recall when Elvis died and my mom wept for the end of an era. I'm sure I'll cry the same way when Jon Bon Jovi dies because his music is timeless. Can I get an Amen?

Unlike the musical tastes of parent and child, the word of God is unchanging. The chorus of his greatness is never shifting. He knows all that has happened and all that will happen, and His promise to be with us always is the truth for generations before us and generations to come.

Like listening to the songs of my youth, I find great comfort in knowing that God remains the same, steady and true for all of His creation.

Never-changing and Ever-loving Father God, in a world that offers no security, I thank You for Your steadfast love, grace and peace. I take great hope in knowing that You know the path that brought us to this day, and You know the path that takes us into tomorrow. Forgive us when we hold too tightly to anything but You. In the name of our eternal savior, Amen.

-8-

It Was Just Summer Camp

But the father said to his servants, "Quickly, bring out the best robe and put it on him! Put a ring on his finger and sandals on his feet! Fetch the fatted calf and slaughter it. We must celebrate with feasting because this son of mine was dead and has come back to life! He was lost and is found!" And they began to celebrate.

Luke 15:22-24

A friend asked me to dinner on that particular Saturday.

"I can't," I gushed. "I finally get Hadley back."

I may have actually choked up a little bit because she responded with a sincere, "Oh no! What's happened to her?"

"Well," I said, dabbing a tear from my eye, "she's been at summer camp. FOR A WHOLE WEEK."

She nodded and said we'd make other arrangements, and I haven't heard from her since. (Not really, but kinda.)

This wasn't even the first time Hadley had been away. She'd been away to several camps, sleepovers, lock ins ... you name it, Hadley's been. She always wants to get away from home … or me … or at least always wanted to go.

The very first time I dropped her off at a sleep over camp, by herself, without me or anyone else I knew, I willed myself to not cry until I was in the dorm elevator. Then the dorm elevator got stuck, and I cried to the maintenance team on the phone.

"Don't be scared," their operator comforted me.

"I'm not scared," I sobbed. "I'm just leaving my baby." Almost an hour later, I was rescued from the hot and stinky elevator and went straight to my car where I might have cried in peace.

When I returned a week later, I took the stairs in the dorm building and greeted my child with open arms … and maybe just a few tears.

Hadley, of course, never understands why there's such fan fare in her (and her sister's) coming and going. She's embarrassed when I hug her a thousand times before leaving, and she's embarrassed when I won't let her go after picking her up.

They'll understand when they have kids of their own.

Hadley (and her sister) also doesn't understand when I get emotional about the other's coming and going.

They'll understand this, also, when they have kids of their own.

My kids aren't going to summer camp to spend their inheritance (although it sometimes seems that way) or to sow their wild oats (this is not to say this doesn't happen) or because they just want out from underneath our roof for a time (but I'm sure this is kinda, sorta the case a little bit). They aren't prodigal children, per say, but, I am a worried parent for sure. I fret about them being in the world, away from me, unable to seek my counsel, tempted and influenced by things I have no control over.

I joke about my time off as a parent, but let's be clear here: No one gets time off as a parent, not even—especially not even—our Heavenly Father.

When we're in this world, we make decisions that sometimes hurt God. These decisions are wild and reckless and, on any day, we could be considered prodigal by some standard.

Yet when we return to our Creator, He welcomes us, showers us with blessings and never wants to let us go.

You're a good, good Father, and You love us more than we can ever imagine. It's always a party when we return to You: whether we've strayed for an hour, a day, or a lifetime. You fret when we are away and never want to let us go when we return. Forgive us for our selfish ways and help us to be considerate of You in all our actions. In the name of our brother we pray, Amen.

-9-

Goodbye, My Friend

By Hadley

For in Him we live and move and have our being.
As some of your own poets have said,
'We are his offspring.'
Acts 17:28

Nothing can prepare us for something as simple as a goodbye. No matter how long I know it is coming it is always difficult for me to say goodbye. We are who we are because of the people in our lives. And when they move, the world couldn't seem bigger and lonelier. They leave a piece of themselves with us and take a piece of us with them.

Growing up in a corporate town, with a branch of ConocoPhillips, I got used to people coming and going as they transfer or are laid off; and until Abi left, they had been just that, people.

It was a few months before school let out when Abi revealed that her dad was being transferred, and they'd leave in early June. I didn't really know what to say. I was sad and already was thinking about how I would get through sophomore year without her in my tribe, but I wouldn't allow myself to be sad in her presence.

The whole time Abi spoke about moving and the new houses they were looking at, she had a genuine smile on her face that reached her eyes, and I couldn't help but smile too. She was so happy about the new possibilities God had awaiting in Texas that I felt selfish about being sad; and I soon found out my friends felt the same.

Within a day of finding out about her move our friend circle created a group chat to plan her a surprise going away party. Complete with her favorite foods, a slideshow of pictures and memes, Just Dance 4, and balloons, we planned it so it would be one of the last things she did in our town, affectionately known as *The 'Ville*. We even added her mom to our group chat to discuss dates. We wanted to end her last week in Bartlesville on a positive note.

It seemed like Abi was never negative, so it wasn't hard to end her time here on a positive note. But I know that like all people, Abi has bad days where she doesn't understand what God is doing for her. So, I put together a Bad Day Box for my friend.

In the box, I added a bottle of her favorite scented bubble bath to help her relax on bad days along with some candles to light in the bathroom to reach maximum relaxation. I also added some sweets and links to some of my favorite YouTube videos I watch when I'm sad. Another object in the box was a journal filled with letters and notes from her friends, track and swim teammates, and even her teachers.

Also included in the box was a letter addressed to 'The Most Positive Person I Know' which explained why I put each of the objects in the box as well as a written remember that God put her in Texas for a reason; He wouldn't move her ten hours away just because. I reminded her to never lose her faith and to continue to grow in her faith and stay positive. The moment she opened the box and read the letter inside was the closest I'd ever come to seeing her cry in the three years I'd known her, and in that moment, I knew she'd be okay.

Even thoughshe's only been there for a month, she's doing great. She's growing closer with her family, has a job and is making new friends. She's already started practicing with her new swim and cross country teams.

Even though I know she's okay, that didn't make the goodbye any easier. So no, nothing can prepare you for a goodbye because there's nothing simple about it. But, it can be an opportunity to lean into Jesus. He goes before us and calls us His own. And that helps me know that together, in Him, Abi and I will be forever friends.

Oh Father, You join us together and You separate us. We don't always understand why or how things happen the way they do, but we want to cling to You and the promise You've made to call us Your own. When we hurt, when we have sad days, when we say goodbye and even when we say hello, remind us that You've put all things in motion for us. In the name of Jesus we pray, Amen.

-10-
Say What?

I tell you that people will have to answer on
Judgment Day
for every useless word they speak.
Matthew 12:36

A late summer night, I sat in the front seat of my friend Harriot's minivan. Our daughters, Grace and Briley, were in the row behind us. We were at Sonic ordering half-price shakes.

When they were handed through the window, the carhop warned us that the lids sometimes slipped off.

"I know!" Grace piped up from behind us. "Once, the lid popped off, and the shake spilled all over the middle between the front seats. You should've heard Mom cuss."

Before I had a chance to even laugh and before Harriot had a chance to defend her choice of words, Briley chimed in. "Oh I know. My mom cusses like all the time. My sister's first word was *damn* because my mom cusses so much. Language!"

Harriot and I laughed at our daughter's confessions and then talked each other out of leaving them on the side of the road somewhere. Bless their hearts.

Also, "damn" wasn't exactly her *first* word, but it was one of her first exclamations after she'd been babbling for a time.

I remember when I was a teen, for the pleasure of my friends and to the shock of my parents, I used to throw around four-letter words like candy. Why? Because I could.

My dad used to tell me to watch my damn mouth when I'd rattle off a string of language, "coloring the air blue".

And now I have a daughter who will toss out a few forbidden words out of anger or frustration. I get it. I don't like it, but I do get it. And believe me when I say this: the weight of hypocrisy bears down heavily on my shoulders every single time I tell her to watch her mouth.

At the very basic level, Jesus was telling us to watch our language in this verse from Matthew. More than that, He's warning us to watch the intent of our language.

Just when we think no one is listening, our kiddos repeat what we've just said. Or worse: They repeat those words as their own. Verbatim.

What is my intent when I use strong language? When I was a teen, it was all for shock. I had an audience with my friends who would giggle at me, I had a mother who would be embarrassed by and for me, and I had a father who would cuss right along with me. It was a perfect cuss-storm.

Now, it's a habit. I typically let my language loose when I'm frustrated or angry or overwhelmed. I'm pretty sure I learned this from my father and possibly my grandmother. As a result of losing control of my tongue, I've taught my daughter to use her curse words in the same way.

Jesus uses the phrase "useless word" to explain that, when our intent is not to share the love of Christ through language, we're speaking in vain.

Just as my high school friends judged me as a funny rebel ...

Just as my young child judged my words as something she could imitate ...

Just as my teenager judged my words as an appropriate response to her frustration ...

Just as my other daughter judged me for having a potty mouth ...

I will be judged by my words. This much is clear. I must choose my words wisely, with the intention of sharing the love of God.

Oh sweet Jesus, You warn us that our useless words will be judged. Yet, sometimes I have no self-control, and the language I speak does nothing to demonstrate the vastness of Your greatness. Forgive me when I cannot use words that bring You glory. Live in my heart and my mind, and guide my words so they are a reflection of the love You have for all of us. In Your name we pray. Amen.

-11-
Keeping Score

But anyone who needs wisdom should ask God, whose very nature is to give to everyone without a second thought, without keeping score. Wisdom will certainly be given to those who ask.
James 1:5

When our daughters were young, I wanted everything to be equal. They were two years apart, so when Hadley started dance, I knew that within two years, Briley would need to start dance. The same rule applied for soccer and eventually t-ball. If one got a piece of equipment or new dance shoes, so did the other.

When I bought one of them a dress, I also bought the other a dress. If we took one of them for ice cream as a celebration, we took ice cream home for the other one.

You know what will happen if you try to keep all things equal? You'll eventually go crazy, and your husband will contemplate having you locked away. (This isn't a bad thought on some days.)

Keeping track of who got what and when and making sure the other had that exact same experience or purchase or reward is ridiculous ... and tedious ... and induces parental insanity.

It also comes back to bite me in the butt when they use it against me.

"But Momma! She got whatever random piece of junky trinket, so I should get something of equal or greater value."

The truth of the matter is this is one (of many!) of my parenting mistakes, but I think we're all guilty of it. We want to give good gifts to our kiddos and often times we think that good means equal.

Life is not equal. Nor is it fair. If it were, no child would ever get cancer, no one would ever starve and everyone would go to bed at night with a pillow under their heads and a roof over their heads. I've not even mentioned a fraction of other injustices.

A few years ago, after being pelted with the *I wants* excessively, I explained I had friends who went on a cruise and that I didn't feel like I needed to go on a cruise. I didn't hate them because they went on a cruise. That's just the way life is. Some people get a cruise, some people get a trip to McGaggles, and some people live on the streets. I finished my metaphor strong, "We need to be thankful for what we have and not look at what we don't have."

I puffed out my chest believing that I had the Mom-Of-The-Year Award in the bag.

Then Hadley yelled for her sister, "I think Mom and Dad are taking us on a cruise!"

Mercy, y'all. If I ask God for wisdom once a day, I ask for it a dozen times.

God is a much better parent than I am. He's much better than Brian is. He's much better than the person who actually does get the Mom-Of-The-Year Award. He doesn't worry about keeping things equal. He chooses to give good gifts, and he chooses to honor us with wisdom when we ask.

The key is we have to remember to ask.

His generosity is documented through the ages when He led his people from Egypt, when He gave Naomi a daughter and a friend in Ruth, when He gave us Jesus to conquer death and bridge the gap between Heaven and Earth.

I do not have all of the answers about raising kids—particularly teenage girls, despite the fact that I like to spout off answers and dictates as if I do. But, I know the One who does have all the answers. He doesn't care if I've already asked Him to guide me through a situation once, twice, or a gazillion times. He doesn't keep score, and He gives freely.

Heavenly Father, who is ever-good and ever-knowing, keep me mindful that You freely give wisdom and want to guide me through this task called parenthood. The gifts You give are wonderful, and You continually give to us when we call on You. Thank You, Father, Thank You. In Your son's name I pray, Amen.

-12-
In A World Of Hurt

You'll receive the same judgment you give.
Whatever you deal out will be dealt out to you.
Matthew 7:2

My precious kiddo survived all the way to her freshman year in high school before she got caught up in girl drama. I count that as a blessing and a curse. A blessing because her middle school years were really, really good by anyone's standard. A curse because she was completely blindsided when a "friend" tore her apart for a reason Hadley didn't understand.

Having confiscated her phone at the end of the tear-filled day, I read through her texts. There was nothing there that indicated Hadley had done anything offensive. There was nothing there that seemed to be a tip off that this attack was coming. It just came.

"I don't know what to do or why she's acting this way," she cried that night as she went to bed.

"Me neither, baby, me neither."

"What do I do?" she sniffed.

The part of me that remembers being a 14-year-old girl wanted to advise Hadley to slander her left and right. I wanted to tell her to reveal every last stupid, dirty, dumb thing her former friend had ever done. Get the upper hand. Push her down where she belongs. Don't be defeated by her crappy way of treating people.

Then, there's part of me that remembers all of my Psych Of The Adolescent college classes. Something—whether it was my child or not—had prompted this. And as much as it pained me, I wanted my kiddo to see the larger lesson of living out her faith. Turn the other cheek (gasp!). Let all that you do be done in love (groan!). Don't judge (grunt!).

They didn't have classes together, so avoiding her would be mostly easy. I say mostly because they had lunch together and sat together in the large commons area.

We devised a plan: Hadley would consider the kind of friend she was looking for, the kind of friend she wanted to be. She would find a person that fit her description of a good friend and ask to sit with her.

It worked out well—but that's her story to tell.

My story to tell is this: I judge harshly ... particularly those who mess with my kiddos. I think all moms do. And if you are the mom of a teenage daughter, you'll have lots of opportunities to judge in this manner.

When I saw my girl's hurt, I judged the one who hurt her. I judged her circumstances, I judged her parents, and I judged the teenager who was probably experiencing a certain amount of hurt herself.

What I should have done, and what I eventually did, was turn all of my attention to my kiddo ... to the one who was hurt. I should have summoned all the love I had to give and showered it on her. I should have immediately surrounded her with my arms and my heart until she felt strong enough to stand on her own. This is what we are called to do not only with our own children, but with all of God's children. And that, my friends, is a tough task.

Amazing God and Father of all, remind us that we are not to judge, regardless of our hurt. We are not to injure or harm in response to someone else's hateful actions. We are called only to love, and it's by that love that we'll be judged. When we love in response to the ill ways of our world, You flow through us and give us a strength that is unfathomable. For that, I am always grateful, and I pledge to remember to do all things in Your love. In the name of Christ our brother I pray, Amen.

-13-
All By Myself

Then the Lord God said,
"It's not good that the human is alone.
I will make him a helper that is perfect for him."
Genesis 2:18

Hadley has taken to her room. A lot. Most times I'll walk by her door and listen to see if I can identify the music she's listening to (lately it's been 21 Pilots) or if I can identify anything else she's doing (typically typing or reading, although I can't hear her reading exactly).

I try to be respectful of her solitude.

Usually.

Sometimes, it's just more than I can take, and I have to knock on the door. In the ~~few~~ ~~dozens~~ hundreds of times I've knocked on her door and peeked in since school has been out, I've encountered the same scene. Her phone is lying beside her playing music. Her computer is in front of her, either tuned to Netflix, YouTube, or Google Docs, and she's sitting criss-cross applesauce with a book in her lap or in her hands. I can tell when she doesn't mind the intrusion because she doesn't growl. Her response is the same, every time, as I peek through her door, "What?"

I plaster a smile on my face and summon up the sing-song voice I used when she was just a toddler and the house was entirely too quiet. "Whatcha doin'?"

"Nothing."

"You wanna come out here and do nothing?" I'll ask, nay beg.

But her answer is always the same: Nope. She'll emerge for meals and when she finds something online or in her book that's fascinating to her or when she finds an interesting lyric that speaks to her, but usually, she just likes her alone time.

Last week, I played the Bible card when she said she didn't want to come out. "But, God said it's not good for humans to be alone, honey!"

She rolled her eyes, "He was talking about Adam and Eve." Sometimes she's too smart for my own good.

I countered, "I'm pretty sure he was talking about moms and kids."

"Get out."

My heart breaks a little bit when I close the door behind me, leaving my kiddo in her bedroom by her own choosing. But, I'm transformed back to a time when I would stay in my room listening to my boom box, waiting endlessly to record my favorite songs from the Top 40 countdown on my clear Memorex cassette tapes. Then, once I'd achieved a recording that had very little of the DJs voice, I'd dance until supper and then dance again until bedtime.

I'm sure my mom's heart broke when I refused to come out of my room because I was perfecting the sweet moves I'd make at the roller rink that week when they'd play, "Out Of Touch" by Hall and Oates.

I know full well that God was talking about creating Eve for Adam when he said it wasn't good for us to be alone. But out of that Adam-and-Eve partnership came children, and children eventually become teenagers, and teenagers eventually lock themselves in their rooms for one reason or another. Maybe it's music, maybe it's silence. Maybe it's movies, maybe it's a book. Maybe it's to escape a sibling, maybe it's to find themselves.

But, when the door opens to my daughter's room, just as I opened my own bedroom door a ~~lot many~~ few years ago, I'll be waiting to be with her. My arms may or may not be open—I'll have to read her face, first.

Heavenly Father, You know being alone all the time isn't good for us, and You give us helpers along the way. You provide friends, family, spouses, and children that walk the path with us. Guide our feet so we walk toward You. Guide our words so we praise You. Guide our hearts so we love like You love us. In the name of our savior Jesus we pray, Amen.

-14-
Necessary Embarrassment

It's embarrassing to even talk about what certain persons do in secret. Everything exposed to the light is revealed by the light.
Ephesians 5:12-13

Hadley needed a dress for her fifth grade program, so we took an evening off to drive to the shopping mecca to the south of us. She picked out a modest dress, but for fun, she tried on a few less-than-modest dresses. She wasn't remotely interested in every wearing them again, but this served as the perfect gateway for me to have *The Talk* with her.

On the way home that evening, in the dark front seat of the minivan, she sat messing with the radio until I reached over and turned it off. I summoned up all the courage I had, took a deep breath and slowly exhaled before I said, "You know, Hadley, your body is changing."

I was greeted with silence. I looked over at her. She was seated, facing front, her back straight, her arms stiffly on the arm rests, her legs at perfect right angles.

I continued my drive as I told her not only about the changes that would happen to her body (eventually) and the need for lotion and shaving and deodorant and bathing, but I told her about changes that would happen to the boys' bodies as well.

Since I was on a roll, I told her, in no uncertain terms, what happens when a man and a woman take their physical relationship to the next level and actually have sexual intercourse. I'll say that again. I used no uncertain terms.

My lecture lasted almost a half an hour. We were almost home.

I glanced over at my daughter and discovered that she had melted into the door. Her legs now bent so that her feet tucked underneath her. Her arms crossed across her developing chest. Her head drooped so that her bobbed hair draped across her face. And, if it were possible, I'm pretty sure she would have put herself between the chair and the door.

"Are you okay?" I asked. "Do you have any questions?"

"Yeah," she said with a cracked voice. "Are you finished talking now?"

I'm pretty sure my method worked for this kiddo. She's shown no interest in boys and is all about academics stating she wants to become self-sufficient before messing with a relationship. Good girl.

My younger daughter, though ... Mercy sakes!

When I finished *The Talk* with her and asked if she had any questions, well ... she hasn't stopped asking them.

I might be a little bit worried about her. Her teachers tell me we have nothing to worry about, but I'm a momma. Why can't I worry?

I love that the CEB uses the word *embarrassing* in this scripture from Ephesians. Even though I spoke eloquently (as much as you can when talking about *S E X* with your kids), it was certainly embarrassing. Briley's questions brought about even more embarrassment.

Despite the embarrassment factor this scripture talks about, it also talks about light: *Everything exposed by the light will be revealed in the light.* That's my prayer for my quiet, introverted Hadley and my loud, extroverted Briley. I plan to expose them to as much of the light as I can and pray for the best as far as the embarrassing things are concerned.

Holy God, creator of all things who knows everything and knows no mystery: Give me strength when the embarrassing things happen. Give me wisdom to choose the right words and the right answers, and give me hope knowing that as my daughters are exposed to Your light, they will remain in Your light. In Your precious and mighty name I pray, Amen.

-15-

Of Picky Eaters And Dirty Clothes

Then Jesus said to his disciples,
"Therefore, I say to you,
don't worry about your life,
what you will eat or about your body,
what you will wear.
There is more to life than food
and more to the body than clothing."
Luke 12:22-23

If ever there were a passage that described our daughters during their early years, it would be these verses. Hadley would no more get up from the table than she'd ask, "What's to eat?" During the time it took me to explain to Hadley I didn't have the energy to answer that question until the dishes from the meal we just finished were done, Briley would have changed clothes three or four times. None of the clothes ending up back in the drawers or in the dirty-clothes hamper.

As a new mom who was sure I was screwing my kids up with every word I spoke, I spent most of my evenings being exhausted worry. Oh, okay, fine. I spent most of my evenings just being exhausted. Worry was a secondary emotion for sure.

Now the girls are older, I'd be happy to tell you they are secure in our parenting and that they no longer worry about meals or their clothing. It'd be a bold-faced lie, but I'd be happy to tell you that none the less.

Hadley, the quintessential picky eater, still worries about what we're eating and when we're eating and where we're eating. She only likes chicken and potatoes and pasta ... and green beans if she's feeling daring. She'll eat some eggs sometimes (but not all the time), and she, of course, likes bread.

Briley still changes clothes, but she usually tosses them onto her bedroom floor as opposed to her dirty clothes hamper. And when she finishes her laundry, she dumps it on the floor, so most days, she changes because her clothes smell dirty, or look dirty, or are dirty.

Truth be told, there are many days when I worry about what to eat. (Will I have time to make it? Will the family like it? Did I thaw out the meat? Why won't they eat this? Who ate the leftovers?) I also worry about what I'm going to wear. (Is this really clean? Is that a stain or a shadow? Does it need ironed? Did I wear this to the last meeting? Why is my blouse in the bathroom? How did this shrink so much in two weeks?)

It's hard for me to tell my girls to stop fretting over their basic needs when I do the same thing. (What's more is that as an adult, I seem to have become more of a worrier. What will happen to my kids if both Brian and I die? Is that man wearing a gun in the movie theater? Who will help them with their math homework if Brian doesn't get home in time? Should I have my cholesterol checked? Was it okay to let the girls stay up and watch *Dateline* just because they were getting along so well?)

The rest of the scripture passage is Jesus telling his disciples that the ravens, who do no work at all, always have enough to eat (kinda like a teenager). So, if God takes care of the ravens, won't He take care of us? He will. I know He will. I believe He will.

But, I'm human. I forget. I worry. I struggle with letting go of my anxious ways.

Just like Hadley, who reminds me every single meal that she only eats chicken.

And Briley, who smells every garment of clothing and asks if it stinks.

Precious Father, who loves us more than the birds of the air and the flowers of the fields, thank You for that love that we cannot even begin to understand. Forgive us when our trust falls short and our worry takes over. Remind us daily that You are in control and the small details of our lives have already been written by You, the author of all time. In the holy name of Jesus we pray. Amen.

-16-
Hashtag: Truth

Cleanse your heart of evil, Jerusalem, that you may be saved.
How long will you entertain your destructive ideas?
Jeremiah 4:14

"I cannot find my biology book, *Mom*!" There was extra emphasis placed on the word *Mom* as if to imply my guilt in the missing science text.

Since she was standing in my room and this was not the first item she'd been unable to find, I asked what might seem like an obvious question, but in reality, was a necessary question. "Have you looked in your room?"

She heaved an audible sigh, threw her hands in the air and proclaimed one of the truest truths I've ever heard her (or any other human) utter. "As if I could find it in there."

No kidding, y'all.

On almost any given day, I could rent her room out to tired parents, bosses, runaways, and celebrities ... anyone who just wanted to get lost for a while.

In all fairness, and since she's standing over my shoulder as I write this, Hadley does a great job of cleaning her room. When the stakes get high (like a missing biology textbook or the blue blouse she borrowed from me without asking is needed), she can make her room look like a congressional librarian came in and did some serious organizing. But, on any other given day, when she's just being a teenager, it looks as if a couple of guys named Vinnie and Tony came in to rough up on someone.

Truthfully, her messy room shouldn't bother me as much as it does. I remember that I once lost my glasses for four weeks. My parents were about to get me a new pair when I discovered them in my bed. They were in my bed! What does that tell you about the state of my room during, what I like to now refer to as, my near-blind stage?

But, now I'm in a precarious position. I'm caught between fully understanding my girl's need to prioritize her life and her room as she sees fit and completely understanding what my own mom meant when she said she didn't want the health department called to our house.

Years ago, prior to becoming a mom, when I just started my teaching career, my principal used to ask a question when we'd send a kid to the office: Is this the hill you want to die on?

I had no idea what he meant at the time.

Now I get it.

The hill is made of dirty clothes, half-eaten slices of pizza and, apparently, lost school books.

Does Hadley's room need cleaned? Yep.

Is her room evil? On most days, the smell would indicate that it is.

Is it destructive? My stubbed toe would like to answer that one for you.

But if a dirty room is all I have to fret over with this child, I'll lay myself on that dirty-clothes hill and take my last breath. My job on earth is done.

It's the other stuff—the stuff of the world, the evil stuff, the drugs, the drinking, the sex, the rock-n-roll—which worry me.

So far, my teen has a clean heart. She's a child of God and wastes no time in demonstrating this through her actions. And that, my friends, is to be desired more than a clean room.

Oh God, my Father, You have gave me a wonderful, although messy, daughter. When I can take the piles and messes no more, point me to the direction of her heart; let me see her as You see her: a work in progress who's not finished growing yet. In the name of my brother, Jesus, I pray, Amen.

-17-
Checking My Momma Self

Preach the word. Be ready to do it whether it is convenient or inconvenient. Correct, confront and encourage with patience and instruction.
2 Timothy 4:2

If the following scene has played out once, it's played out a zillion times in the past few years:

Daughter does something I don't think she should.

Me: What? That's so wrong!

I don't remember my parents being so opinionated on the way I should act.

Now, let me be clear. They had standards. They had expectations. But, I recall being allowed to make mistakes and—here's where it gets tricky—live with those mistakes. My parents were quick to step in when I needed them to correct my behavior, to tell me how to make it better, and then they pushed me on down the path called life. From what I can tell from stories and my own husband's behavior, I believe his parents were much the same way.

I have no idea why we have become parents who demand expectations of perfection from our own kids.

I could blame the internet. I could blame the fact that, as a society, we want all of our interactions to be Instagram-ready. I could blame social media, 24-hour news stations, and blogs that are easy and swift to remind us how much we are lacking. Truly, I tell you, my kids have never had a tooth fairy pillow and their baby teeth will not be made into a charm bracelet to be given to them at the announcement that they'll be parents themselves.

Or, I could, as I was taught, take responsibility for my own actions.

What exactly is my job as a mom? Is it to dole out punishment? It's what I seem to do most, and it's exhausting. Is it to point out every single mistake my kiddos make? The trouble with that is sometimes I get so in tune to their misgivings that I overlook the things that make them wonderful and beautiful and brilliant little creatures.

This is not how my earthly parents treated me. It's certainly not how my Heavenly Father responds to me.

Yet, in trying to do what's ~~right~~ perfect, I've gotten it all wrong.

Do you ever feel this way? That you've done not one single thing right as a parent? I feel this way on a daily basis. Parenting is hard, y'all.

Or is it?

It feels hard, but I think it's only hard when we're doing it wrong.

I've been instructed in Second Timothy, to correct, confront and encourage.

It's hard, though. These girls of mine are fearless (for the most part). They like to stretch their minds and their bodies and soar often, even when I'm not ready for them to.

My goal is to ignore that which says I'm not perfect. Clearly, I'm not. (My girls will attest to that under sworn oath.)

My goal is to preach The Word.

My goal is to correct them but also encourage them.

My goal is to raise them to be world-changers being led by their Heavenly Father.

I hear You laughing, God, when I think I've got this parenting job down. You, as the prime example of how to correct and encourage, should be my model and my standard, not the blogs and pages and writings of the world. You and You alone are sufficient for me and for our children. Guide us. Correct us. Confront us. Encourage us. Always, dear Father, always. Amen.

-18-

Sisters ... Unchanged By Time

By contrast, Martha was preoccupied with getting everything ready for their meal. So Martha came to him and said, "Lord, don't you care that my sister has left me to prepared the table all by myself? Tell her to help me." The Lord answered, "Martha, Martha, you are worried and distracted by many things. One thing is necessary. Mary has chosen the better part. It won't be taken away from her."
Luke 10: 40-42

If you have a sister, you've related to Martha way too many times. You've done all the work while your sister sat around watching MTv (or whatever was popular when you were growing up). There was also a time when you were accused of being Mary—sitting at the feet of whatever was important to you at the time (the Mickey video by Toni Basil, maybe?) while your sister just griped, moaned and complained.

And if you're raising sisters, then, Mercy. Bless you beyond measure. I'd say that we identify with The Lord, but the truth is we find ourselves in awe of Him because how in the world? How did He remain calm? How did He refrain from sighing heavily and muttering under His breath about holding it together so that human services doesn't come relieve Him of His parental duties? Or something like that.

Sisters are funny little creatures, though. I recall wailing on my sister until she was in tears over a Cabbage Patch Doll whose ears I wanted to pierce with a safety pin and then the very next day, being mad at my mom for making my sister cry when she was told she had to eat at least two bites of peas. How dare she make my sister upset in that manner!

Best of friends and worst of enemies, indeed. Sisters: the original *Frienemies.*

Then, because my mom is a powerful pray-er, I'm assuming, I ended up with a pair of sisters to raise.

In a moment of mom-weakness, I threatened to call human services on myself after a particularly intense sister fight. I was convinced they'd stand more of a chance to make it in this life if they were not under our roof. Within two minutes of my empty threat, both of my daughters appeared at my side begging for clemency for the other.

"But, Momma! She's my best friend!"

"Momma, please don't send her away! She's going to teach me to braid hair! I love her!"

With tears in their eyes, the epiphany hit: They were talking about the other, and the fight was back on.

"She's calling for *you*, dumphat."

"You are the one she's sending away, itch with a B."

I lay on the bed, one on either side of me, my phone on my chest. How did Jesus do it, really? If there were any doubt this man is also holy, one only need to see how He held it together in the presence of fighting sisters.

Take care, Moms of sisters, though, that's not the end of Mary and Martha. Later, their brother became ill. Together, they sent word to Jesus to come to them. They both kinda chastised Jesus for not arriving sooner. Then, when Jesus raised Lazarus, the sisters were grateful, once again, for their friendship with the Lord.

The gospels certainly did a great job capturing the crazy that is called sisters. They don't say exactly what Jesus's response was to their actions and complaints, but I can't help but think that maybe He smirked a little bit and quite possibly rolled His eyes.

It's the news that, in the long run, sisters will band together for the better part. They will not be distracted. They will sit at the feet of the Savior and listen to His message.

Jesus, I don't know how You did it most days. On those days when they won't sit still and they won't stop arguing and they won't stop turning my hair gray, take my hand. Guide me to a better place. Remind me there will come a time they will seek You, hopefully together, but I've got to let You lead me as I parent them. In Your name I pray, Amen.

-19-
Beauty Is Itchy

So don't throw away your confidence—
it brings a great reward.
Hebrews 10:35

I could not wait until I got my ears pierced (my dad's rule was I had to wait until I turned 12) and until I got to wear make-up (also when I turned 12—it wasn't the magical age he made it out to be). I saved up all my birthday money (which was like ten dollars), and I bought myself some blue eye shadow, blue mascara, some concealer and some Bonnie Belle lip gloss. My mom and dad paid for my ears to be pierced as their birthday gift to me.

Man! I was styling.

Even though my affinity for blue eye shadow hasn't waned much, my desire to look somewhat, kinda-sorta-half-way decent is still alive and well. So, when Hadley, my older daughter, was about to turn twelve, I told her she could start wearing make-up. I even said I'd pay for it ... and not even call it a birthday present.

She thought about it for a moment and then shrugged me off with a pleasant, "No thanks."

No thanks?! What prepubescent, tweenage girl doesn't want to wear way more make up than is appropriate?

Now, let me be very clear. I didn't think, nor do I currently think, she needs any kind of beauty assistance at all. This lack of desire to enhance her beauty was foreign to me, though.

She wanted to get her ears pierced at an early age (at my prodding), and I gave in. In an odd series of events, our dog is to blame for accidently pulling the first set of earrings out. The second set of earrings got infected. After that, Hadley said earrings really weren't that important to her. I agreed to not pierce her ears again until she honestly and truly wanted them pierced. That was ten years ago and she still has no holes in her head that weren't put there by God Himself.

Every once in a while, I'll ask if she wants her ears pierced. She politely declines citing she doesn't have the time to deal with them at this juncture in her life.

A couple of years ago, she decided to give mascara a try. She's got gorgeous dark auburn hair and her eyelashes have a tendency to go lighter instead of darker. She thought the eye goop would be just enough accent for her eyes.

"Do you want eye liner? Lip gloss? Blush? A blush brush?" I peppered her with questions as we stood in the cosmetic aisle. She was looking at mascara. I was looking at everything else.

"No," she said carefully pulling her selection from its perch, "Just mascara, thanks."

Within a week, I noticed her mascara tossed in the bathroom drawer instead of its usual plopping place beside the sink. I carried it with me to her room.

"Are you still wearing mascara?" I asked as I examined her eyes closely.

"No," she said matter-of-factly. "It itches my eyes and, besides, I don't think I look like myself when I have it on."

I have no doubt that there will come a time when vanity will win and she'll buy all the latest cosmetics.

In the meantime, though, I've had a paradigm shift myself. If this kiddo, excuse me, young woman, can combat the forces that have their sites trained on her adolescent insecurities and win, who am I to stand in her way with promises of making her beautifuller? (Pretty sure that's a word.)

I'm not willing to give up my blush or eyeliner—it's been my constant companion for many, many years now. But, I am willing to stand more confidently in the fact that my Heavenly Father created me beautiful and confident. And I shouldn't doubt that He'll reward me for my confidence when I stand before him ... in my original face.

Holy God, You've made all things beautiful. Forgive us when we fail to see the beauty in others and in ourselves. Show us we need nothing more than the gifts You've given us. Grant us strength to stand before others as children of our Heavenly Father. In the name of the Holy One we pray, Amen

-20-
Feed. The. Dogs.

Imagine a brother or sister who is naked and never has enough food to eat. What if one of you said, "Go in peace! Stay warm! Have a nice meal!"? What good is it if you don't actually give them what their body needs? In the same way, faith is dead when it doesn't result in faithful activity.
James 2: 15-17

Hadley and Briley were born not only to Brian and I, but to Daisy as well. Daisy was the sweetest, most gentle fur sister any kid could ask for. Toward the end of Daisy's life, through a comedy of errors, we ended up with Bo and eventually, after Daisy's passing, Jesse Jack, or JJ.

(We had an escape artist of a dog for a while named Luke until he found his way to his next family. For those of you who were 80s kids, you've already figured out Brian was a big fan of *Dukes of Hazard*. This is why Brian was not given much power in choosing our kids' names.)

I always took care to feed and water Daisy daily, brush her regularly, and calm her fears during thunderstorms and fireworks. When Bo joined our family, I convinced Brian that an extra dog would be a good way for the girls to learn some responsibility and learn to care for another living thing.

Hadley, who was in first grade, proudly announced since she was going to be a veterinarian, she'd take care of Bo and teach her little sister to do the same.

This lasted for exactly thirty-six hours.

Since that exact moment, I've spent my days begging the girls to feed the dogs, brush them, and give them fresh water. They like to do fun stuff, which is to say they like to pet them and, and then complain about how demanding I am when they think I can't hear them. On occasion, they feed the dogs without my incessant nagging. These occasions are typically to show the other one how much better she is than the other.

Nonetheless, the dogs love whoever brings them food and pets them. Dogs are fickle that way.

Recently, Hadley got up from the table, put her plate in the sink, stood at the back door promising she'd feed and water the dogs in that sing-song voice we all use when conversing with our pets, then promptly went to her room and shut the door behind herself.

If the dogs were able, they'd eat our food at the table with us. This is why they stay outside during meal times.

If they had opposable thumbs, they'd freshen their water throughout the day. They'd probably also spray water at each other.

If they could read weather maps, they'd come in before the storm arrived.

If they understood calendars, they'd hibernate under our beds from June 30 – July 5.

But, those things are pretty much impossible for them to do; they are reliant upon us to take care of them.

Some things are also impossible for some children of God. Not every person has enough to eat. We must feed them.

Not every person has clothing. We must dress them.

Not every person feels secure in this world. We must comfort them.

Not every person knows God. We must be His hands and feet, His love and His embrace.

Creator of all things, Father of all people, Hope of the world: Nudge us, nag us, remind us daily that we are entrusted to care for our friends who cannot care for themselves. In our pathway, You've set the task of feeding, comforting and loving each other. Let us be ever mindful of the blessings in our lives and to share those blessings with those we encounter. In the name of our Lord we pray, Amen.

-21-

Three Years

Then Jesus said, "This is what God's kingdom is like. It's as though someone scatters seed on the ground, then sleeps and wakes night and day. The seed sprouts and grows, but the farmer doesn't know how."

Mark 4:26-27

"Mom ... in three years I'll be leaving for college anyway."

I have no idea what we were talking about. I recall we were in the car, and I almost slammed on the brakes in the middle of the road at the realization that Hadley was right. In three years, she would be graduating from high school and going to college.

Ya know ... if I don't decide to lock her in her room make her take online classes.

How did we arrive at this point? How did my nine pound, six ounce baby girl become an almost six-foot tall high school sophomore with whom I could have intelligent conversations? How did the last fifteen years speed by like traffic exiting the big city on a Friday evening?

Three years.

She was right. She would be graduating in three years and making adult decisions. She would be deciding what she wanted to do with the rest of her life. She can make friends without the benefit of her mom and dad vetting them for her. She can choose when to go to bed, what to eat for dinner, when to wash her sheets, whom to go out with, how to spend her money ... in just three years, she's be an independent creature. Mostly.

How much life can change in three years.

Just three years ago, she was starting middle school and complaining about her summer reading and wanting to make sure she had all the right school supplies ... not just for her teachers, but for her friends as well. (Bic Felt Markers are huge with the middle school crowd.)

Three years before that, she stopped reading the Harry Potter series because she heard rumors that some of her favorite characters wouldn't survive until the end.

Three years before *that,* she independently walked into her pre-kindergarten screening and blew them away by counting to 149 before they made her stop.

And now she's talking about leaving for college in three years.

All along her life's journey, as well as the life's journey of her sister, we've prayed with them. We've made sure they understand their obligations to their Creator are to love Him and love others. We've encouraged them to serve others, to seek God, to ask for forgiveness, to extend grace, to show mercy ... to reflect the love of Jesus in everything they do.

In three years, when I'm not around to nag her about being good, being smart, doing what's right, she'll have to make those decisions on her own. I'll have to see if the crop we've planted in her will sprout and grow. In three years, I'll have to let her go into the world while I pray for the best.

She's confident; she's ready.

I'm not.

But, I have three years, to continue to nurture the seed that is scattered within her heart. A lot can happen in three years.

Heavenly Father—I don't know how You did it. You sent Your only son into our world knowing He would be crucified. I pray my child has a privileged life, but I still want to hold her close to me. Give me strength and peace as I slowly send her into the world. Bless the harvest that is within her so Your love is reflected in her life and she lives so that others come to You. In the name of Your son, Jesus, Amen.

-22-

Ready and Willing to Go

By Hadley

"Have I not commanded you? Be strong and courageous. Do not be afraid; do not be discouraged, for the LORD you God will be with you wherever you go."

Joshua 1:9 NIV

Last summer I was given the opportunity to travel with a team from my church to Red Bird Valley in Kentucky. I was the youngest missionary by nearly ten years, and, because of this, my mom gave me every opportunity to back out. Yet I was determined to serve on this mission. I'm not gonna lie, I was skeptical at first about serving with so many that were nearly thirty years my senior, but, looking back, I wouldn't want it any other way. I learned so much from these pro mission-trippers, Red Bird leaders, and even those in the small Kentucky community.

One of the biggest lessons I learned at Red Bird was to go with the flow. Often, we didn't have a plan until we got to our work site, and most of the time, we didn't know where our work site was until we got there. During my week at Red Bird, I worked at three different sites each one with a task vastly different than the one before and the only thing we could do was adjust, and for me that was difficult.

I've been a planner my whole life; I plan out trips that haven't even happened yet and could possibly never happen. It's been a natural part of my life, but when I got to Red Bird, I had to completely change my mindset. And thinking about it know, it was probably the best thing to ever happen to me. Since I've come back, granted it's been a very small change, I've been slightly more spontaneous, and I don't plan everything out. It's freeing!

Although mission work was such a major part of my time at Red Bird, what is still most prominent in my mind is our team's nightly meetings. After dinner, after alone time, after naps and showers, we met on the porch which connected our cabins and just talked. The majority of the conversation topics were about our work from earlier in the day; our group seemed to be able to talk about anything, from children to jobs to retirement, and, sometimes, even my high school experience so far. But no matter where our conversations strayed, we were always lassoed back in for nightly devotions and the telling of our "Jesus Sightings". We spoke of the actions of our fellow missionaries and told stories of the humorous mishaps of the workers.

My time in Kentucky was very short-lived, as I was only there for a week, but the lessons I learned and bonds I built will be present throughout the rest of my years. This being my first mission trip, it has opened many doors for me in my church. I'm now the youth representative of our Outreach Committee and have been given the opportunity to serve on an international mission trip to Costa Rica. After my time serving on this mission trip, I've become more active in the church and have learned to spread God's love everywhere I go.

Because the adults surrounding me had a heart for God, they taught me how important service and mission work are.

I realized in that week, I hadn't truly known Christ. I knew about Him, but knowing Him came when I was serving others in His name, who others who have the gifts of mission.

Jesus opened my heart to missions during this week. I plan on taking this love with me around the world. I don't know that I'll make missions my livelihood, but I will be certain to continue to serve in this capacity throughout my life.

Jesus, brother and servant, thank You for the opportunities to serve others in Your name. What a privilege it is for us to act as Your hands and feet so that others can clearly see You and feel the love You have for each of us. Make our hearts open to the opportunities to minister every day. Keep our hearts open to know You through Your people. In the name You, who first served us, Amen.

-23-
Brace Face

Focus your eyes straight ahead;
Keep your gaze on what is in front of you.
Proverbs 4:25

Through a series of unfortunate events—school testing, strep throat, a mix-up in calendars—Hadley's appointment for getting her braces on ended up being postponed by almost six weeks.

Out of exasperation, she lost it at the orthodontist's office when we showed up on the wrong date. "Why can't I just get my braces on?" she practically screamed once we were in our car and with a mouth still void of anything metal.

It did seem like we'd been trying to get her teeth on the straight and narrow for quite some time. Her teeth were not terribly out of shape, so to speak. In fact, the ortho assured us that she'd be a brace face for no more than a year.

Most kids I'd known in my twenty-plus years as a middle school teacher didn't want braces. I didn't understand why Hadley was so bent on getting them immediately if not sooner.

"What's the rush?" I asked as I put the correct appointment date into my phone.

"Mom," she sighed as if having to explain the world's secrets to me for the umpteenth time, "the sooner I get them on, the sooner I get them off."

Well ... yeah. That made sense.

But this wasn't exactly how we tacked most dreaded tasks.

I don't like to wash my sheets. I like clean sheets, let's be clear about that, but, I don't like stripping the bed, washing the sheets and remaking the bed. It's a task that exhausts me. Therefore, I put it off very last. Sometimes, I'll even let the sheet washing go an extra week or two or six.

Briley doesn't like to brush her hair. She'll put it off until her hair is basically dry and then she'll throw it in a ponytail or a bun and call it good. It's a rat's nest to be sure, but she's gotten out of brushing her hair. So, in her eyes, it's a win.

And, of course, I'm guilty (as is everyone in my home) of hitting the snooze button numerous times. It's so much more pleasant to wake up when we want to instead of when we have to. This causes lots of tardiness, much yelling and cursing first thing in the morning and breakfasts that consist only of plastic wrapped American cheese. Only.

Hadley, however, has taken a different approach with her braces. She wants to face it head on and get it over with. She wants to walk the path she has to walk as swiftly and ably as she can to reach her goal ... which in this case is straight teeth.

Eventually, we were able to get our scheduling act together long enough to get her in the orthodontist's chair and get her pretty turquoise brackets on. We learned how to brush and care for her torture devices. We were sent home with a t-shirt, lots of coupons and free samples and a great big bill. But, she had her braces.

In retrospect, I'm grateful for her willingness to bite the bullet and jump into braces with both feet. I'm hoping she'll learn to face undesirable tasks this way at all times.

I'm also grateful for a Savior who didn't postpone or delay the inevitable: His crucifixion.

I'm grateful He invited Judas to the Passover meal, knowing Judas was instrumental in our salvation.

I'm grateful He didn't try to hide from the Roman soldiers who came to arrest Him.

I'm grateful He didn't bargain with God for three more weeks or five more minutes. I'm grateful He kept his eyes on the straight path and looked at what was in front of Him: Salvation for the world.

Jesus, when it's so easy for us to put off tasks or meetings or jobs that are not desirable and, perhaps, messy or maybe draining, remind us that You willingly faced Your own death to offer us salvation. You've set a straight path in front of us and given us eternal life to focus on. We just have to walk toward You and encounter all that is before us. In Your name we pray, Amen.

-24-
Go Girl!

Instead, we are God's accomplishment, created in Christ Jesus to do good things. God planned for these good things to be the way that we live our lives.
Ephesians 2:10

My friend, Alyssa, and I talk about our girls a lot. Her daughter Emma and my Hadley are in the same grade. They are both as sharp as cheddar, have a wicked creative side and are embraceable introverts. (But don't try embracing them.) Neither went to the winter formal at their school because why dress up to hang out with a bunch of people you may not know? Their words, not ours.

They are good friends with each other and write for the school magazine together—both being the first freshmen to be selected for the school magazine. (Totally shameless mom-brag right there.)

They are just as different as they are similar. Emma speaks French, Hadley Spanish. Emma is very science-y while Hadley loves history. Emma likes to read science fiction, and Hadley loves to curl up with a good, realistic fiction.

We have good kids. They have lofty goals and the skills to take them wherever they want to go.

This, however, doesn't stop me and Alyssa from worrying about them endlessly and trying to push them achieve more. To do more. To be more.

"If something happens to me," Alyssa texted me during one very serious health crisis, "make sure Emma goes to at least one formal and help her get a good dress."

I assured her that I would that I'd take a lot of pictures, and that I'd be on Emma to do all the things Alyssa wanted her to do like white on rice. (This is punny since Emma is Korean, and I'm Caucasian.)

Another time, I texted, "I need Hadley to join the following groups: Honor Society, Service Club and Flashing Club. Those are the ones that she'll enjoy the most."

Alyssa texted back that I needed an intervention. "I get wanting her to join stuff, but flashing?"

Spanish ... autocorrect makes a mess of most of my messages.

We plan for, wish for, worry about, pray with, fret about, brag on our daughters no less than three or four times a day. If anyone were to ever confiscate our SnapChats, text messages, Instagram pics, or smoke signals, one could assume that we had no other hobby.

Funny thing is this: Regardless of how much data we use preparing our older daughters to finish high school and to bolt into the world (please, God, don't let them hibernate in their dorm rooms), it doesn't really matter.

I mean, sure. We have a huge influence on our kids—perhaps the heaviest influence they will ever know!—but God has created them for great things, despite us.

Despite their mothers? Oh man, yes.

Before we even held our babies in our arms and dreamed big dreams for them and cried real tears for them and made a mental list of twenty-zillion-bajillion things we had to teach them before the world got a hold of them, God created them to live a good life. He created them to do good things.

At some point, we'll just have to let them do those good things without discussing those actions with at least a half-a-gig of data. We also have to know that God created us, as mommas, to do good things. Don't believe me? Look at your own kiddos.

Created in You, Jesus, we are set on a path of good things. All of us—even the children that will always be our babies no matter how tall they grow or how far they move away. Keep us mindful that our children were Your children first, and the miracle of their lives is not only a reflection of us, their earthly parents, but of their Heavenly Father as well. In Your holy and good name we pray, Amen.

-25-

Get Out Of Bed

Wake up and strengthen whatever you have left,
teetering on the brink of death,
for I've found that your works
are far from complete in the eyes of my God.
Romans 3:2

Emily's sweet girls, Gracie, Eva and Caroline, are younger than mine. While we are staring down high school graduation in a few short years, Emily is just beginning the journey as an elementary school parent with a preschooler under foot and a baby wrapped to her.

Late one night, she confessed that she'd just had enough. She sent her girls to bed in the middle of an activity. She just needed the break.

Oh my goodness. I felt her so intensely. There were many nights when I'd get home from school and barely get dinner finished before I was bathing my girls and putting them in bed.

We are human, after all, and our patience does wear thin. Sometimes it's justified; the kids are crazy and wound up, and we do need the break because we can literally hear our brains ticking like a time bomb. Sometimes we're just feeling off and, you know as well as I do, that when Momma's off, everything's off.

Putting our kids in bed early, even if it's only because we need the silence and we need it right.this.very.minute, is okay.

Usually, we can take a moment in silence, take a cool drink, sit still without being touched and feel right as rain with just a few deep breaths.

I can remember vividly those times with my own girls. My heart broke for Emily as she admitted she just needed the break. The guilt in her voice over being human was tangible.

"Gracie asked me what she'd done wrong when I tucked her in," Emily confessed.

I thought back to the nights I'd sequestered my own girls to their rooms.

"Go get her out of bed, read a book with her. You'll feel better," I offered not so much as advice but as an offering of regret on my own part.

Can't we always see clearly the things we should have done? As a mom, I feel like the times that I've felt full of regret are often spotlighted in my memory. I don't readily recall the times I put the girls to bed at their regular times, read them books, prayed with them. But, I can easily recall the times I put them in bed just a few steps ahead of losing my sanity.

When I advised Emily to go get Gracie out of bed and read with her, I knew then, beyond the shadow of a doubt, if I could go back and take my own advice, I would do it.

I'd go back to the time I came home grumpy from a bad day at school and couldn't shake the grump for my girls. I'd pile them in bed with my husband and me and read *I Love You All Day Long*. I'd sing "Say A Little Prayer." I'd scratch their backs longer. I'd listen to them drag out a two-minute story to twenty minutes. I'd seek their forgiveness sooner rather than later.

Emily texted me shortly and said Gracie announced it was the "best day ever." I cried for her. There's nothing more reliving as a parent than to hear your child proclaim their love for you in whatever words they choose.

Teetering from the brink of death is the phrase the scriptures use, Father. More times than we are comfortable with, we feel that way as moms. The promise is You have a greater plan for us. When we're weary, let us be quick to forgive ourselves and to wake up to the wonderful things You've placed in our lives. In Your name, Jesus, in Your name. Amen.

-26-
Shhhhh! Don't Tell

God's eyes are on human ways,
and He sees all their steps.
Job 34:21

After a particularly rough day with Hadley, I attempted to teach her, at the age of three, about the value of confession.

That night, as she went to bed naked (because she refused to wear any pajamas) with a dirty face (because she snuck chocolate milk after I'd told her to go to bed), I lay down beside her and began my lesson.

"You know," I said, "when we do things we shouldn't do, we need to tell someone about it." In my simplistic, amateur-parent mind, I just knew she'd come right out and tell me what I already knew: She'd rubbed me raw.

"So," I continued, "tonight, we're going to tell God about the things we shouldn't have done. I'll go first …"

The following is not an exact transcript of the night time prayer we said that night, but it comes pretty close.

Me: Dear God, Thank You for loving us.

Hadley: And thank you for my family.

Me: Sometimes, God, we do things we aren't supposed to do.

Hadley: But not always.

Me: But sometimes. Like I shouldn't have snuck an extra bite of casserole after supper.

Hadley: Amen.

Me: Nope. It's your turn. You tell something you are sorry about.

Hadley: Nothing. I'm not sorry about anything.

Me: You know what? I'll tell God, then.

Hadley: [clapping her hand over my mouth] Just don't tell Him everything.

Y'all? In all my years as a human being who loves Jesus, I can't even think of a better way to sum up how we feel about our own confessions!

I can remember being in sixth grade confirmation class with my friend Kristin. We decided to skip over the "forgive us our trespasses" part of the Lord's Prayer one evening. We felt like we'd had a pretty good day and didn't really need to be asking for forgiveness when none was needed. As if it were a commodity that God rationed.

(We also sang "All Women" instead of Amen at the end of the hymns because we were 80s ladies and pretty full of our feminist selves. But that's another story. Ahem. Where was I?)

It's cute when a three-year-old sneaks chocolate milk from the fridge and drinks it standing behind the sofa. It's obnoxious when a teenager decides she has nothing pressing that needs confessing. But it's exhausting as adults when we don't confess. Without confession, we hang on to the guilt, the deed, the knowledge. God offers us forgiveness freely, but it's hard for us to hold that forgiveness close to our hearts when we're hanging on to the things that are weighing us down.

I've snuck my fair share of chocolate (though not the milk) as an adult. I've refused to wear many garments for a variety of reasons. And there are very few moments in the day when I don't think I shoulda coulda woulda been a better mom or wife or friend if …

Confessing our sins—our trespasses—to our Heavenly Father. He's already seen us do that offensive act. He's witnessed our wrongdoings. He already knows all of it. Confessing is saying that we admit it and we're tired of holding on to it. We want to free our arms for the grace and mercy that Jesus is ready to give.

Thank You, Father, that You already know everything we've done and love us despite it all. You want to give us Your grace. You want to give us a spirit of forgiveness. You want our arms to be empty of sin so we can hold tightly to You. Forgive us. Love us. Hold us. In Jesus's name we pray, Amen.

-27-

Passion vs Fuss

His disciples remembered that it is written,
Passion for your house consumes me.
John 2:17

There was a time when Hadley, my older daughter, wouldn't agree with me if I paid her good money to do so. It seemed like it lasted about three decades, but in reality, it was only a few seasons with a relapse or two here and here.

During one particular fussy evening (to put it nicely), I asked her to unload the dishwasher.

I know. But wait. Hear me out before you call human services on me for such an inhumane request.

Brian and Briley were out of the house doing something softball related, I'm assuming. My mom was in rehab after her knee replacement, so the house was quiet with just the two of us at home. I had some laundry from the dryer in the basket and headed back to my room to fold it. I stopped at Hadley's room and knocked on her door.

"When you get a moment," I said, "Could you please do your part of the dishwasher? I'll do your sister's part."

Normally, I don't do anyone's part but mine, but I needed to load those things from the sink that had been soaking for a little over thirty-seven thousand hours.

I walked on to my room, hearing Hadley's door jerk open behind me. Before I could even set the laundry basket down, Hadley was giving me a list a mile long as to why I shouldn't do her sister's chores.

Every time I tried to interject my reasoning (such as this task needed to be done a.s.a.p. because there was a fungus growing in our sink that would probably interest NASA), Hadley would come again with an even more impassioned reason as to why she was a poor urchin child and her sister was a pseudo-glorious princess.

Seeing that I would never get a chance to say anything, I just let her ramble. I folded the clothes as if I weren't even listening to her rant. Eventually, Hadley left me to finish my laundry and when I walked through the kitchen, I noticed both racks of the dishwasher were empty.

I don't fault her passion over inequity. In fact, my deepest desire is she'll continue to fight for justice in our world as she matures and enters adulthood. We could use more of her kind fighting for fairness and equity.

And I don't want to say that her fight was misplaced. In her mind, it was very important that her sister learn to do her fair share. I couldn't agree more (even though I didn't get a chance to tell her that).

Truthfully, I expected to see the dishwasher still completely full when I went back to the kitchen.

I don't know why she opted to do her sister's part of the dishwasher, but I'm grateful and told her so, receiving a grunt in return.

Her arguments have become more logical and her passion has been more appropriately placed since that time. Her rants (and my often times rant-y responses) have become less and less. Our talks have a developed more conversational tone.

But, for one brief second, I caught a glimpse into the passion that I want her to have about being a child of God. I saw clearly the passion we are called to have for the kingdom of God ... the passion we are to have when God's will is not being respected ... the passion we should have when we care for all of God's creation.

She's still fussy (just ask her about the plight of homeless families or the large gap of wealth distribution in our world). She can still fire up a good rant (I'm hoping her lawyer salary will pay for a nice retirement villa on the beach for her parents). I hope she still wants to right wrongs. She has a beautiful vision of how our world could be. I'd empty dishwashers from now until the end of time to see that vision come to be.

Father, the hardest part of parenting a strong-willed child is keeping her passion alive while guiding her to a more appropriate form of expression. My parenting and my leading must come from You and You alone. You've given me this child and equipped me to be her mother. My job is to be patient with her as she develops a passion for You and Your house. In You name I pray, Amen.

-28-
Throwing Glasses

Conduct yourselves with all humility, gentleness, and patience. Accept each other with love, and make an effort to preserve the unity of the Spirit with the peace that ties you together. You are one body and one spirit, just as God also called you in one hope.
Ephesians 4: 2-4

I sat all day long in the living room. Hadley was in her room, my mom in her room; Brian and Briley were gone, as usual, to a softball scrimmage for most of the day. It was a truly lazy day, but I spent it in our familial common area and not one word was spoken to me. In hindsight, I now realize I should have taken that time to clear my head and write. But, that's not what I did. I continued to stream episodes of *The Office* by myself.

Eventually, when I decided it would just be an alone day, I retreated to my office. My office is actually just a little alcove off of our bedroom. There are no walls or doors that separate it from the rest of the space.

I sat down, put on my reading glasses, cued up iTunes and opened this document. Within two minutes—I know because I looked at the clock on my screen—both daughters and my husband were in the room, all gathered on our bed, discussing homecoming, dress up days, European history homework, pitching lessons, and general other discussions that could have taken place two minutes earlier at the very least.

They'd call out to me for my opinion but wouldn't necessarily wait for my answer. It was a distraction to say the very least. Wait ... *They* were a distraction. I haughtily closed the laptop and threw my glasses onto my desk. I swiveled in my chair to face them full on.

It was at that time that no one had anything more to say.

Upset by my fit, all three of them stomped off and retreated to their own private space, leaving me to feel completely guilty for wanting ten minutes of alone time to write a devotion for this book.

I kept my glasses on my desk and my laptop shut and slowly went to them, one at a time, to make amends.

It's so hard to explain "me-time." It's necessary for a clear mind and an even temperament and a spirit that's welcoming and loving. But, taking time for myself is filled with guilt most days.

I'll confess: This is not the first fit I've thrown. This is not the first time I've needed to seek out my family in order to ask their forgiveness.

Being a mom and finding time to maintain your own sanity is akin to walking a tightrope with no training, no net, no balancing bar to keep you walking straight and also? You're wearing a blindfold and people are yelling at you, sometimes throwing things.

As a mom, you will fall. Paul's letter to the Ephesians instructs us to conduct ourselves with humility, gentleness and patience. He was talking about being a general part of the body of Christ, but isn't our family also a part of this same body? And yet, I threw my glasses and huffed around. Maybe Paul was writing to me. That Paul is a wise one.

I still believe all mommas need their alone time. It should be mandated that children not bother their mothers during certain times of the day (to be determined by the mom, because c'mon! We need to feel like we're in charge of something!).

However, when that alone time is compromised, and my head is still clogged, and I feel as if I'm about to fall from the tightrope, I need to keep these words in mind: God called us in *one* hope. I should shut my laptop softly, place my glasses down gently and join my family on my bed. My alone time will come later. Right now, they need their momma.

Father God, this is hard for me and so easy for You. You receive calls for Your attention in every moment, and yet, You are patient with us. I get huffy when my time is interrupted. I need the break, yet You never leave us. Forgive me. Guide me to make better choices and to use my time more wisely. In the precious name of Jesus Christ I pray, Amen.

-29-
When Giving Up Is Your Best Option

Crying out in a loud voice, Jesus said,
"Father, into your hands I entrust my life."
After he said this, he breathed for the last time.
Luke 23: 46

Hadley was bitten by a dog. It was not an attack. It was done in playfulness. The dog belonged to our neighbor, and we'd played with him a dozen times. It was just a very unfortunate accident. Her eyes and nose were only scratched—Thank you, Jesus. Her lip, however, had a half-inch gash in it.

The ER was crazy busy for our smallish city. Two heart attacks, a stroke, and a shooting came in after Hadley did and took precedent over my kiddo's split lip. Around 11 p.m., they came in to stitch up Hadley's lip. In order to line her lip-line up, they would be knocking her out with a very dangerous drug. I say dangerous because most people will wake up in 15 minutes remembering nothing about the procedure. But one in ten-thousand people will never wake up. The drug had, at some point, been used in executions. Essentially, it would disconnect the nervous system for a short period. In fifteen minutes, it would reconnect.

They administered the drug, I watched her eyes roll to the back of her head as her eye lids fluttered and her fingers and toes twitch. The doctors quickly sewed up her lip in a matter of minutes. And then we watched the clock, waiting for her to wake up so we could go home.

Fifteen minutes.

Twenty minutes.

An hour.

A nurse was assigned to sit in our room. Her vitals were now being taken every fifteen minutes.

It would appear that my baby—the sweet girl who made me a momma—wouldn't wake. She'd be the one in ten-thousand.

After two hours, I closed my eyes and gave my child to Jesus. I prayed that I'd rather Him take her now than to see her lying in a hospital bed for the rest of her life.

"She's Yours," I breathed.

The rest of the night was spent watching my child, then watching the monitors, then watching my husband—weary and praying his own prayers—then watching my child some more. "I Surrender All" echoed through my brain, acting as a dam, holding my tears at bay.

Shortly before six, I thought of how easy it seemed for Christ to give Himself up for us, how easy it seemed for Him to comply with His Father's commands, yet how difficult it must have been for God to watch His only Son's life be betrayed and stolen and removed from this earth. I closed my eyes, the tears leaking out despite my protests and began my prayers all over yet again. "Take her, Jesus..."

And then she woke up. She sat up and took up the fight against the shot she'd been given just six hours before, just like they said. That was ten years ago—despite a tiny little scar on her upper lip, you'd never know she had any kind of health issue ever.

How merciful is a God who spares our children daily. How full of grace and peace is He when our children leave us despite our most fervent prayers. How holy is He that He allowed His son to be sacrificed for us.

Our most holy and gracious heavenly Father, when we pray to You, You know exactly what we feel and how we feel. There's nothing we go through that You don't know about already. Thank You for your endless amounts of mercy and grace and holiness that You grant us with every breath we take. In the name of Your son who sacrificed His earthly life so that we could gain eternal life, Amen.

-30-

A Grand Entrance

Our mouths were suddenly filled with laughter, our tongues were filled with joyful shouts. It was even said, at that time, among the nations, "The Lord has done great things for them!"

Psalms 126:2

Hadley learned to walk when she was nine months old. We expected her to crawl; instead, she pulled herself up and began walking. Our lives as we knew it was over. She was a bundle of energy and she wore us completely out.

So, Sunday mornings, when other moms opted to keep their children with them until Children's Moment, I didn't even hesitate to put Hadley in the church nursery from the get-go. Our church at the time was a fairly small church, and there was one nursery class. So, most Sunday mornings, the nursery attendants would bring the children from the nursery into the sanctuary for their own special time. Once Hadley was walking, I would've bet good money that they brought her in because they needed the break.

But, an interesting thing happened once she could walk. She'd politely and daintily hold the hand of the nursery attendant as they made their way to the back of the church, waiting for the hymn to end. She'd look around, smiling at all the somewhat familiar faces. And as soon as the song stopped, she'd break free from the grasp and bolt into the sanctuary, laughing the whole way.

She'd often times wave and holler out "Hi! Hello!" to her church family. She'd head to the choir and visit with the choir members. She adored the church pianist who would often times actually let her play a few notes during the children's moment. Then, when the minister would offer his closing prayer, Hadley would take that as her cue to return to the nursery attendant and eventually to the nursery.

Now, lest you think I was a free-range, *laissez-faire* mom in letting her have her run, please understand that I spent a good eight weeks chasing that kid all over the sanctuary, willing myself to not cuss aloud as I crawled over the laps of church leaders in pursuit of my little rebel.

Every single person we apologized to would sincerely counter with pleas of us to not worry about her antics. People seemed to enjoy the comedic relief she offered during our time of worship.

But, it was one gentleman I'd known all my life that tempered my temper. As I chased after her one Sunday, he grabbed me by the arm, stopping me in my pursuit. He pulled me into the seat beside him, put his arm across my shoulder, and leaned into me.

"Leave her alone. We should all enter the Lord's house with that much enthusiasm."

For the rest of the children's moments, I watched her race up and down aisles, high fiving and hugging people. Sitting beside that wise friend, I watched her hug legs and kiss knees. I watched her giggle with joy with someone would "trap" her between. I watched her make her way around the sanctuary with nothing but pure joy on her face.

I also watched the faces of those she passed by light up. They didn't steal her joy; instead they shared in it; if anything, she freely gave it to them.

More times than not, especially since becoming a mom, I've entered worship with a stained blouse and a scowl on my face, already planning my Sunday afternoon nap. Hadley has, of course, grown and is now a teenager. She doesn't always enter anywhere (much less the sanctuary) with joy in her heart. But, not a Sunday goes by that I don't recall the day a little child—my little child—and a wise old man taught me that laughter and joyful shouts are a very important part of our worship.

You have done so many great and wonderful things for me, my God. How insulting of me to enter Your sanctuary with anything but Your joy on my face. Forgive me when the things of this world wear me out and steal the joy You've given to me. Remind me daily that entering Your house as a joyful toddler is the way I'm called to enter into Your presence. Thank You for your filling of my soul. In Your holy and joyful name I pray. Amen.

-31-

The Unseen Score Book

If we live by the Spirit, let's follow the Spirit. Let's not become arrogant, make each other angry, or be jealous of each other.
Galatians 5:25-26

"Aren't you going to get onto her?" one kid or the other will generally and bitterly ask while the words of their own disciplining are still hanging in the air.

Typically, we try to discipline our kiddos in private; however, as with most things in a family who lives in one household, there are no secrets.

The thing is, we have two very different kiddos when it comes to taking their lumps.

Hadley—the older child—is very vocal. She keeps track of every single time we take away her phone (which is more of a punishment for us now that she's in high school but not yet driving), every time we turn off Netflix, every time we tell her no on any given subject. She's loud and recounts every time she was wrongly imprisoned and her sister was not. She probably has an Excel spreadsheet.

And that brings us to Briley, Hadley's sister, the baby of the family. When she is disobedient, she quietly receives her consequences, hands over her phone, stays in her room, gives up her iPad ... whatever she's been sentenced to. Thus, her quiet acceptance leads to two things: First, it irritates her sister and gives her sister the impression that whatever her offensive deed was, it has gone unpunished. Second, she's so timid in her acceptance, we never check up on her for compliance. And typically, she'll snag her phone back before it's time or sneak a view of Netflix without us noticing.

Sometimes I think we're raising future leaders ... of prison gangs. Their fifteen minutes of fame will be for quietly organizing and carrying out a prison riot.

I'm kidding.

Mostly.

As their ~~probation officer~~ parent, the follow up is pretty telling. Hadley's main complaint is that her sister isn't punished as Hadley saw fit. Briley's main complaint is that she didn't know she's supposed to give up her iPad for everything; she thought it was just for YouTube ...

Hadley's problem is she's too concerned with vengeance on her sister, and Briley's problem is she's too concerned with cheating her way out of punishment. Both of these are completely and utterly normal responses for teenagers who've been justly punished.

"It's easy," I've told them both on several occasions. "Take care of yourself." I remind them *c o n s t a n t l y* that their only job in relationship to their sister is to love her.

But, I know it's hard.

I want justice in this world. Probably more than that, I want justice for me. Often times (mostly on the evil playground called social media), I have no problem telling others what their problem is or quietly doing what I want to do even if it's not what's right. C'mon! Don't tell me you've never "forgotten" to log that extra piece of cake or glass of wine on My Fitness Pal.

If we choose, instead, to allow our eyes to be focused on Jesus, allow the spirit to be our only guide, what a beautiful difference it would make not only in our lives but in the world.

Paul's words to the Galatians are an invitation: Let's live by the Spirit.

It's hard, but it's worth it. I'm in ... are you?

Holy God, whose spirit is ever-inviting us to abide in You, thank You for the call. Forgive us when we don't accept and chose, instead, to seek out our own path, to cheat ourselves and others, to pay more attention to the faults and injustices found in others than in using our flaws to come closer to You. Continue to call our name, Holy Spirit. Continue to invite us to a rich and focused life in You. In the name of Jesus, Amen.

-32-
It's Not *That* Bad

When times are good, enjoy the good;
when times are bad, consider:
God has made the former as well as the latter
so that people can't discover anything that will
come to be after them.
Ecclesiastes 7:14

One wild and crazy Saturday as I was doing the laundry, our dryer became noisy. Like really noisy. It sounded as if someone had dumped about seven dollars worth of pennies in the barrel. I just shut the door to the laundry room ... and the door to the kitchen, which is connected to the laundry room ... and I hid in our bedroom with music blasting through my ear buds.

When the dryer finished (as evidenced by the deafening silence), I went and collected my still damp laundry.

Laundry's not supposed to be damp straight out of the dryer, so I put two and two together, whined to my husband, and loaded up the girls and all the laundry in the house and headed to the Laundromat.

While my husband stayed home trying to set up a service call, Hadley, Briley and I, along with every quarter in the tri-state area, set about washing all the laundry from our house.

Our shared time together was not without complaint. I tried to encourage them to look around and see the diversity of their fellow launder-ers. They pointed out there was an older gentleman who was washing an all-pink load.

I encouraged them to take in the scents that are not necessarily available in our well-ventilated laundry room. They pointed out a well-ventilated laundry room was, indeed, a blessing.

I encouraged them to use their brains and find a way to get happy in the dirty clothes they were wearing. They, in turn, patted their pockets down looking for their phones.

It was at that exact moment, Hadley made a horrible discovery. She didn't have pockets. If she didn't have pockets, her phone couldn't be in them. If her phone wasn't in them, it had to be in the car. But, her phone wasn't in the car, and that clearly meant that she had no method of self-entertainment.

Unless ... you consider the fact that her phone could be in one of the washers that we just loaded. And what could be more entertaining than digging around eight full washers of sudsy water?

The phone was retrieved and seemingly ruined. Hadley declared the Laundromat the worst place she'd ever been. She declared the day to be the worst day ever. And she declared all of it my fault.

Of course.

As I stared at the man with the all pink load (it was neon, hot pink, y'all, not red-sock-in-whites pink), I told Hadley in no uncertain terms she could get glad in those same pocket-less clothes and she'd better do it before the buzzer on our washer sounded.

She was quiet for a moment with her soaked and sudsy phone in her hands. I could almost see her brain going through the cycles and slowly a smile spread across her face.

"We have insurance on my phone, right?" Indeed we did. Way to find the silver lining, sweet girl.

It's so easy to get caught up in our own selfish emotions that our thinking and judgment becomes as cloudy as a sudsy washer tub. When we stop, breath deeply and set our mind to finding the good God has placed in our lives, we can take any situation and turn it into something worth a smile.

P.S.—The sound that sounded like seven dollars worth of pennies? It turned out to be seven dollars worth of dimes. So, our service call was only $70 instead of $77.

Good and Gracious God, You have given us good things for our own enjoyment. Forgive us when we fail to find the good and only concentrate on the bad. Keep our minds and our hearts focused on You, who have blessed us more than we can know and nudge us to share good with everyone we meet. In the name of Jesus we pray, Amen.

-33-
D

Go to this people and say:
You will hear, to be sure, but never understand;
and you will certainly see but never recognize
what you are seeing.
Acts 28:26

I left town to attend an education conference the day after D was reported as missing. He was in Hadley's class, and my husband and I had both been his teachers in seventh grade.

In the past year, he'd run away before but had always returned home by bedtime. He'd been gone for more than twenty-four hours when I left.

Tuesday morning, his body was discovered; D had taken his own life. I texted Hadley throughout the day, knowing it was against school rules, but believing my colleagues were going to be understanding as the kids found ways to cope with their friend's death. Tuesday evening, I was still at my conference when Hadley called me. She was aware of the affinity I'd had for this sweet kiddo and his precious spirit, and she wanted to make sure I'd known about his death.

She also needed to process it.

"I'm just so mad!" she growled as I tried to melt into the phone so I could be with her, see her, touch her, hug her.

"What makes you mad, honey?"

"All these people who are now claiming to be his 'best friend' for starters." I couldn't see her, but I imagined her using air quotes around the term best friend. "Plus, he had a rough life, and it seems that from the beginning until now, he just couldn't catch a break."

"I know." Mercy sakes how I knew. He'd been one that had touched my heart and pierced my soul from the first day I met him. I swallowed hard.

She continued, "I don't think he knew how many people really cared for him, and I guess I just don't understand a lot of it ... or any of it."

I sighed. She is so smart. And here she was on the phone with her older, but not much wiser mother. "I don't understand either."

I explained many people have ten thousand more friends in death than they do in life. It was no consolation. I tried to explain that, sometimes, rough lives are what some people are given through no fault of their own. It didn't take away her anger or frustration or sadness.

Finally, out of misery or exhaustion or maybe just weariness of talking about it, Hadley said, "We'll probably never understand."

See? I told you: She's wise.

I have no way of explaining so much that happens in this world to my kiddos. I can use the clichés such as *everything happens for a reason, God needs him in heaven*, or *whatever will be will be*. These are clichés for a reason: They are tiresome and meaningless.

And, truth be told, it's hard to explain things to kids that we don't fully understand ourselves.

In the case of D, I refuse to presume I know what was going through his head or what had crushed his heart as he made that final decision on this earth. Our lack of understanding is just one of many things that make us different from our Heavenly Father. What I do understand is God loves us more than we can ever fully know. I don't have all the answers. It's frustrating to me and to my kids (and quite often my husband as well). And as a momma, the message of God's great love is what I do know and what I want them to fully understand.

We are hurting. We don't understand. But God's love is greater than anything else—even when we cannot see it or understand it.

Father, send Your Spirit to comfort us and to grant us peace. There are many things that surpass our understanding, there are many things that break our hearts and crush our spirits. At those times, allow us to be open to Your Spirit and to rely on You as we learn to go on with life through the changes. In the name of Jesus Christ we pray, Amen.

-34-
Momma Is A Groupie

God made the nations so they would seek him,
perhaps even reach out to him and find him.
In fact, God isn't far away from any of us.
Acts 17:27

My friends from our small group at church and I went to the Belong Tour. I set out to go because Jen Hatmaker and Shauna Niequist were going to be speaking there and in my fantasy world, they would spot me in the crowd and ask me to sit down to dinner with them.

We volunteered at the tour because it would be a fun way to meet people and get the conference paid for.

And ... as I learned later—I swear it was later!—we got to possibly meet the talent. That's backstage speak for Jen Hatmaker and Shauna Niequist.

In addition to Jen and Shauna (hereafter referred to as my BFFs), JohnnySwim, a husband wife musical duo were going to be performing as well. When Hadley found this out, she blew a gasket because JohnnySwim is her favorite musical performer ever. Exclamation Point.

As luck would have it, I got to meet my BFFs: Jen on Friday night for a picture opportunity and Shauna the next day at her fan meet-and-greet. They were both great! I actually got to visit some with Shauna, retelling parts of her book back to her that impacted me. I hoped to get to visit with Jen as well. But ...

She was scheduled to have her meet and greet at the same time as JohnnySwim.

Gulp.

Momma was going to have to make a decision.

The night before, Hadley tweeted out how unfair it was that I was getting to hear JohnnySwim while she was stuck at home. And JohnnySwim favorited it. Exclamation Point. Exclamation Point. Exclamation Point.

So, all day on Saturday, I received texts from Hadley asking about their concert, what songs they played, what they were wearing, how they looked, how they sounded, if I thought it was fair that I got to hear them when she didn't ...

During their meet and greet time, I gave up my time with Jen to meet JohnnySwim. I recalled the thousands of texts from Hadley and mentioned her text.

"We remember her!" they exclaimed. "Where's your phone?"

Then, on my phone, they made her a minute-long video telling her that they missed her, and they'd look for her at a future concert. I was over-the-moon ecstatic. Hadley was going to flip! My friends were excited for me and for her. I still love my BFF, Jen, but missing her for that video was worth it. (Sorry, Jen! Call me!)

And I was right: Hadley flipped. She was beside herself with giddiness and immediately looked up their concert schedule. She was a fan for life. Exclamation point. As was I. Exclamation point.

It had been a while since I sought something with such passion and had gotten so excited over an event or an occurrence. It was a big deal, and my desire to meet some heroes was strong.

On Monday after I had returned home, I thought about the weekend with a smile. I showed the video for Hadley to everyone who said hi to me. It was going to be a hard weekend to top.

I wonder what our lives would be like if we sought God with the same fervor. I wonder how the world would change if I exuded the same passion about the way in which Jesus has blessed me. I wonder how many people, like the 10,000 ladies who didn't get to meet Jen, would be over-the-moon giddy with all kinds of Exclamation Points if someone, including myself, told them about the wonder and love that is our God.

Sometimes our passion and excitement needs some focus. And some Exclamation Points.

Holy Father, Your love excites me. Your blessings encourage me. Your mercy and grace embrace me. Let me never grow tired of seeking You with passion and excitement. And let me never grow weary of telling all who will listen about the goodness that is my God. In the name of my savior, Jesus, Amen.

-35-
The Text In The Middle Of The Night

If one of you wanted to build a tower,
wouldn't you first sit down and calculate the cost,
to determine whether you have enough money
to complete it?"
Luke 14:28

Sundays are my favorite days. Typically, we get to leisurely prepare for church, go out for lunch afterwards, take a nap, prepare for the week. I said typically.

On some occasions, when we have a softball tournament or have traveled or experienced some other random occurrence, our Sundays are hectic. Many times, these Sundays find us scrambling for clean clothes to start the week with. More often than not, Hadley is the last one to do her laundry. Don't feel bad for her. She likes it that way. This means she can leave her laundry in the dryer all week long and never have to fold it. She's a smart cookie.

It was about two in the morning on a Monday after one of those hectic Sundays that I got a text. Initially, I wasn't sure what woke me up. But, I got up and went to the bathroom anyway ... because I've reached that age where I need to go to the bathroom every chance I get. When I returned to bed, I noticed my phone's light fading. With much anxiety and trepidation, I checked my phone. Middle of the night contact was never a good thing.

I grabbed my phone, took a deep breath and swiped my thumb. The text was from Hadley: Will you put my clothes into the dryer when you wake up?

What? I read the text again. Sure enough: At two in the morning, she was sending me laundry reminders. I walked down the hallway, my phone in hand, to Hadley's room. Opening her door quietly, I fully expected to see her still on her phone. She was seemingly asleep. Seemingly. I continued my walk to the laundry room where I took her clothes from the washing machine and put them into the dryer, making sure to turn the machine's alarm off before I journeyed back to bed.

If typical Sundays are my favorite days, then typical Monday mornings are my least favorite days.

When our alarm sounded, we hit snooze no less than a half-dozen times and then scrambled to get ready in time.

"Ohmygosh, Momma!" Hadley belted out from her room. "Did you change over my laundry?"

"I did!" I hollered back, "Why didn't you do it before you went to bed?"

"I fell asleep before the washer was finished," she called back from the bathroom she shares with her sister.

"Then why were you texting at two?" I called as I stood in my closet wondering what to wear.

"That's when I remembered about it," she yelled a muffled yell, her toothbrush probably in her mouth.

As a mom, I hope my children will leave our home prepared to budget their time, their money and their talents. There's no guarantee of that—I know! I am one of those kiddos who's still learning to budget those things even now!

But, I also hope that they'll learn to see a task through. I hope the foundation for their tower of faith will not be kept empty. I hope they invest in their spirits and their souls and their faith's journey. I hope they budget the resources to keep on the path I've set them on. I hope they see their relationship with God as an ever-moving living entity and not just a one-time a week Bible study.

And, like the two-in-the-morning text, I hope they know they can call on me when they are feeling lost or stalled, just as I call on our heavenly Father when I need fluffed up.

Holy Father, who has set us on a path that leads to You, renew us so that at all times and in all places, we are building ourselves up for a relationship with You. Guide us in our budgeting so that all of our resources bring us closer to You. And when we find ourselves stuck, remind us that on easy Sundays, hectic Mondays, morning, noon or night, we only need to speak Your name to find You and Your help. In the name of Christ we pray, Amen.

-36-
Even Her

Offer prayers and petitions
in the Spirit all the time.
Stay alert by hanging in there
and praying for all believers.
Ephesians 6:18

Hadley was looking forward to her weekend. She was excited about being away from me and her daddy—she's leaving for college in just a few short years, as she enjoyed telling us. Her sister, however, was going with her on this particular weekend, much to Hadley's chagrin.

Our youth group was taking their annual camping trip to a beautiful (and unplugged) state park; the kind where they'd have to hike to the bathroom and rely on a battery-operated flashlights once the sun set.

The day they were to leave finally arrived, and the girls packed and loaded the car. I drove them to the church where they met with their friends and youth pastor and adult sponsors to drive to Arkansas. We made a quick stop to grab some snacks. At this stop, Briley, my younger daughter, remembered that she forgot her jacket at home. With plenty of time, and a promise from Evan, our youth pastor, they wouldn't leave without the Davis sisters, we headed back home so Briley could get her jacket.

When Briley ran in, Hadley huffed. "Why does she have to go?"

"It's her youth group, too," I reminded her.

"Yeah," Hadley puffed, "but why does she have to go with me?"

I reminded her God provided a space and a place for them to be together. "See what you can learn this weekend with your sister. Maybe there's a lesson in it for you."

"I doubt it," she sighed. The huffing and puffing grew more tiresome.

"Pray about it and see what God decides to show you," I encouraged her as her sister, jacket in hand, returned to the car.

I glanced at Hadley to see her roll her eyes before shutting them and turning her face to the outside.

We arrived at the church with plenty of time. The girls unloaded the car and giggled with their friends. Parents took pictures of the funny campers knowing full well the kids who returned to us in seventy-two hours would be a lot more tired and a lot less clean.

Hadley avoided her sister. When Briley and her friends her age would wander too close to Hadley and her friends, Hadley maneuvered herself to the opposite side of the group.

It was my turn to roll my eyes. One day, when I was long gone, they'd appreciate each other.

I glanced at Hadley again and our eyes locked. She made a bee-line for me.

She leaned into my ear and said, "Mom, I forgot my sleeping bag at home."

I grinned, told Evan we'd be right back, and we set out for home. Again. She arrived back at the church just in time to toss it in the back of one of the sponsor's trucks and climb into the church van.

Sometimes, when other believers are our sisters or some other irritating person, it's very hard to pray for them. It's hard to hang in there when we're feeling discouraged by the circumstances or by having to share our space with those people. But, when we pray for them, God changes us. Sometimes the change comes from an observation. Sometimes the change comes from a situation, and sometimes that change comes when we can see ourselves as we see others.

God of all things and people, show us clearly that You have ordained our times and spaces. You have given us people in our lives who can teach us lessons, who can pray for us and who can let us see You in a vibrant way. Forgive us when we allow ourselves to get in the way of a relationship You've given us. In Jesus's name, our brother, we pray. Amen.

-37-

Roll With It, Baby

Many plans are in a person's mind,
But the Lord's purpose will succeed.
Proverbs 19:21

"But you said we could go to Ron's," Hadley's little voice said when we told her that we were going home after dance class instead of next door to our favorite hamburger joint. She, of course, was not eating a burger but would eat chicken instead.

"Well," I consoled her, "we can't now. We need to run home."

"But, Momma!" she complained, her voice rising to the occasion, "I had my whole night planned on eating at Ron's."

As I write this, I cannot recall why we didn't eat at Ron's that evening. But, I remember thinking how in the world could our change of plans mess with a three-year-old's plans. That's right. Hadley was just three years old at the time.

She's always been a planner. She announced at the age of five that she did not appreciate surprises when we tried to take her to look at Christmas lights one weekend without telling her exactly where we were going.

When she was in second grade, she decided it would be best if she didn't go to school because there would be a substitute teacher, and she wasn't sure that the sub would follow the plans to the extent that Hadley would want her to.

In fifth grade, she wrote social studies lesson plans.

The kid is nothing if not a planner, and we've known this since she was born, which just happened to be on her due date—no kidding.

While the stories of a toddler having her evening ruined because of a change in dinner plans are pretty humorous, there's a not-so-funny side to this. The sub in second grade didn't follow plans and Hadley ended up trying to get the teacher and the class back on track. As you can imagine, it didn't work. Rarely does it work when a seven-year-old decides to take matters into her own hands. She came home feeling like an exhausted, friendless failure.

As she's grown, her desire to have a plan for everything has often robbed her of happy, serendipitous moments. This has led to Hadley having a greater level of anxiety than the normal teenager.

At three, we could convince Hadley that eating chicken nuggets at home was just as good as eating popcorn chicken at Ron's. As a teenager, some frozen chicken nuggets rarely do the trick. We have to not only calm her fears, but reassure her that a change in her plans is not the end of the world.

Most planners are not just about knowing the plans but also controlling those plans. This is also true in Hadley's case. When her plans change, she feels very much like she's lost all control.

The hard lesson for her to learn (and for us to teach her) is God has all the plans and all the control that is ever needed. When she frets over a delayed test or a change in weekend plans or a new friend or a different situation than she envisioned, she robs herself of the joy of the situation.

The good news is God wants the best for us. We need to push our own plans off to the side, dig into our Bible, spend time listening to what God has to say, and allow God's purpose to take over.

Great and wonderful Father, thank You for the plans You set in place for us. Comfort us when we are nervous, guide us when we are confused, and remind us that Your plans and purposes are so much better than any we could ever imagine for ourselves. In the name of our perfect Lord we pray. Amen.

-38-
A Host of New Grandmas and Grandpas

Love each other like members of your family.
Be the best at showing honor to each other.
Don't hesitate to be enthusiastic—
be on fire in the Spirit as you serve the Lord!
Romans 12:10-11

Hadley joined Instagram at thirteen after a summer camp in order to keep in touch with her fellow campers and counselors. She joined Twitter to follow her favorite politicians (no lie), but she joined Snapchat (after some very well-defined ground rules) to keep up with her friends. And, sometime after her fourteenth birthday, she joined Facebook. I'm not sure what her motivation was because when I asked if she wanted to make a profile, she scoffed at me.

But, when she joined, she friended both her daddy and me, so I felt confident that, whatever her motivation, it was benign if she was allowing us in as "friends".

I cautioned her to not spam people with a lot of "do this if you love me or him or them" type posts, and she cautioned me to not stalk her. I reminded her people were very brave behind a computer screen, and she needed to let us know if she were ever harassed on Facebook or anywhere else for that matter. She reminded us that she knew what to look for. Even though she seemed to have it under control, I patrolled her page pretty religiously and very thoroughly. I watched what pages she liked and which people she friended. She was a good online citizen.

Then, something odd happened this summer. There came an influx of older-aged friends on her Facebook. Some of them I knew from church, and some of them I didn't even have one single friend in common with.

"Honey?" I started one afternoon, knowing I needed to tread cautiously lest she block me. "You need to be careful about friending a lot of people. Just because you know them one hour for one day a week doesn't mean you should friend them. They might not appreciate being spammed with friend requests."

"Like who?" she asked, her defenses up.

So, I pulled up her profile on my phone and began naming names.

"Mom," she interrupted me, "they sent me a friend request. I just accepted."

"Really?" I asked, feeling like I needed to turn in my social influencer card at the blogging convention.

"Yeah," she answered, "we all went to Red Bird this summer. They're my mission family."

Ahhhhh ... this summer when she went to Red Bird Mission, she was the youngest missionary by several years.

The mission trip was not only a construction trip, but it was also a cooking and sewing trip—perfect for those retirees who wanted to contribute something to those less fortunate. And for a kindhearted teenager!

Her week away from us with twenty other believers changed her attitude about the way in which she was privileged. It also opened her world to the "family" she has within our own faith community.

Our heavenly father has placed people in our world and in our lives in order for us to share the journey with them. Hadley was fortunate enough to meet a whole dynamic of God's children that she might have not considered as friends otherwise. Her enthusiasm is exactly how God wants us be toward each other.

You are a good Father who has blessed us more than we can even imagine. Perhaps, one of Your greatest gifts to us is the people You've given to us. Help us to fully appreciate them not only as Your children but as the family You've called us all to be. In the name of our brother, Jesus Christ, Amen.

-39-

The Value of a Value Meal

As surely as I live, says the Lord God,
not even your sister Sodom and her daughter did what you and our daughters have done!
This is the sin of your sister Sodom:
She and her daughters were proud, had plenty to eat and enjoyed peace and prosperity,
but she didn't help the poor and the needy.
Ezekiel 16:48-49

It was a few weeks from Thanksgiving when my daughters and I drove out of our neighborhood onto the main thoroughfare of our town. As I slowed to make the turn, I heard one of my daughters whisper to her sister, "Lock the doors." Without any hesitation, her sister, riding in the front seat, obliged. I glanced to the passenger seat, wondering what happened that would cause them to lock the doors ... and then I saw him.

He appeared to be dirty, probably homeless, holding a sign that read, simply, "Hungry."

My heart broke. I want my girls to be cautious, of course, but I also want them to be compassionate.

"Why did you lock the doors?" I asked as I drove to the closest McDonalds.

"Momma," one of them offered, "we don't know him."

“Plus, he was dirty,” the other offered in a rare show of support.

Without telling them where I was going, I talked to them of compassion, how most people would choose to have a home and a job and be self-sufficient, but that wasn’t always possible. “It’s up to us to help them when we can,” I explained as I turned into McDonalds and drove through, ordering a value meal, a coffee, and a soda along with a fried apple pie.

“Are we going to take it to him?” they asked. Even though I’m sure they knew the answer, their voices didn’t hide their concern.

When we returned to the spot where the man was, he had moved from the corner. The girls breathed a sigh of relief, even though I’d told them they didn’t have to get out of the car if they didn’t want to.

“Who will eat his food?” one of them asked at the same time I spotted him. He was standing against a police car, handcuffs binding his arms behind his back.

Now it became my turn to allow my concerns to take over my intentions.

I recognized the police officer as a friend I had gone to high school with and decided to follow through with my intentions of feeding the hungry, taking care of the needing, loving the unlovable. I pulled behind the patrol car, much to the dismay of my daughters, and grabbed the cup holder with the two drinks along with the bag with his fast food in it. Then I got out of my vehicle.

The officer was putting him in the back seat, his hand on the top of the homeless man's head.

"Hey!" I interjected. "Ummm ... this sounds silly, but can he have this food?"

Chris checked his watch and said, "Actually, it'd be good. He's already missed dinner tonight." He took the food and drinks and placed them in the front seat.

"Can I speak to him?" I asked, wanting my girls to see it wasn't bad speaking to either the police officer or the homeless man.

"Sure. He just has a failure to appear. It'll get him off the street for a day or two and give him meals at the very least."

I bent down into the doorway. "I don't want you to think no one cares," I started. "And I hope and pray that this is a turning point for you and better days are ahead."

He nodded his head, smiled and said, "God bless you."

Funny how that works out: I intended to bless him and teach my daughters a lesson about taking care of those less fortunate. Yet, he just blessed me and my girls. Mercy, God knows how to teach us a lesson, right?

Holy God who loves all of his creation and his children, continue to teach us the lessons You'd have us learn so we can live in harmony and peace with all of our brothers and sisters. Amen and amen.

-40-

A Big Wave

The one who supplies seed for planting and bread for eating will supply and multiply our seed and will increase your crop, which is righteousness.
You will be made rich in every way so that you can be generous in every way.
Such generosity produces thanksgiving to God through us.
2 Corinthians 9:10-11

"What's a tsunami?" Hadley leaned into me and said one morning in church as our mission director spoke of Japan's needs following the 2011 tsunami.

"A big wave," I whispered back, still wanting to hear more about ways we could help. Our church gives through The Advance directly to UMCOR, United Methodist Committee On Relief. Japanese officials, fearing for the safety of their citizens on the relatively small island, requested funds and supplies but no workers. Our church was taking up an offering; the children were taking up a noisy offering, asking the adults to donate all of their change into metal containers. It was noisy but effective.

"I want to give some money," ten-year-old Hadley whispered back to me. "Give me your money."

I, however, had not brought my purse, and Brian had only brought his debit card. I explained the situation and told her we'd bring money the next week, knowing full well that one day's worth of offering wouldn't meet the need of the country.

"So, this week can we make some earrings to sell?" Hadley proposed.

After our trip to the beach the summer before, we learned to make earrings, bracelets and necklaces, seashells serving as our main beads before advancing to regular ol' beads. That week, after getting approval from the mission director and the pastor, we got busy making more earrings. After church on Sunday, we sold our earrings so Hadley could donate to the tsunami relief. She donated $400 that day.

Later that spring, a tornado hit a small town in our state, Tushka. The tornado ran its course less than forty miles from her grandparents and her aunt and uncle.

Again, Hadley made some earrings and sold them. Again she donated all of her proceeds to the tornado relief. She took great pride in using her skills to make something worth selling. She also took great pride in being able to give money—her money—to help others.

She was interviewed nationally for her mission heart and her desire to give. At ten years old, she recognized the impact of giving. "Think of how much better the world would be if everyone did something." Without even reading the words of Ezekiel, she knew that God would provide what she needed in order to help others.

Generosity is ingrained in us. God created us to be in a relationship not only with Him but with each other. Part of that relationship is giving of ourselves, our talents, and our excess to those who are in need.

Think of how great our world would be ...

Glorious God, allow us to have Your people, Your will, and Your spirit guide our actions. Keep us mindful that You supply our needs so we can be generous in our giving. Forgive us when we fail to see how much better our world would be if we gave through our blessings. In the name of Jesus Christ we pray, Amen.

-41-

More Shushing

The ear that listens to life-giving correction dwells among the wise.
Proverbs 15:32

After church, we were at our favorite Mexican restaurant. It's an added bonus that it's next door to our church home. There were five of us at the table: Brian and Hadley sat on one side of the table facing my mom, Briley and me.

Saturday had been an extremely stressful day. Brian and Briley were out of town at a softball tournament. I planned to go as well, but my mom had fallen back against the toilet and cracked the toilet tank. I spent Friday night cleaning up the draining tank and Saturday morning trying to convince a plumber that we needed him immediately if not sooner.

Hadley had a babysitting gig later and wanted to go to the Christmas open house at her favorite shop. Once the plumber left, I spent the rest of the morning and early afternoon taking her around town and then to her babysitting job before my mom and I headed to the softball tournament. I got to see one game, and Briley, a pitcher, wasn't in the rotation that game since she'd pitched the game before, which they won.

We headed home, and I visited with a friend who was borrowing our laundry room to complete her family's weekly laundry. Her plumbing lines were backed up and awaiting repair.

That night, because I didn't drink nearly enough water during the day, I was up probably four times walking off cramps in my legs.

Exhausted yet? 'Cause I am just writing about it and I can promise you that I was worn out smooth after that day. If we hadn't committed to bringing breakfast to our Sunday morning small group and if Hadley hadn't been the helper in children's church that morning, we'd have probably all slept in until our bodies woke up naturally. (My natural wake-up time is not in the morning.)

Sunday's service, All Saint's Sunday, had us lighting candles to remember our church family who had passed away that year. We also lit candles to remember those others in our lives who have gone before us. I can't remember exactly what Pastor Jeff spoke about that Sunday, but I do remember singing the words to "Holy Spirit You Are Welcome Here" on repeat in my head. I might have been in a slight worship-song coma due to exhaustion.

So, on Sunday after church when we were all sitting around the table at *Sabores*, I know for a fact I was having a hard time tuning in to the goings on around me, specifically (apparently) at my own table.

When Hadley said she needed silverware and Brian teased her with her silverware (which was at his place setting), I tuned in just in time to hear Hadley growl, "Give me the silverware. I'm done with you."

It was just enough to set me off. My mom-lecturing voice turned on, and I proceeded to give a lecture about growling, respect, family, tone of voice, elders, children, parents, kindness, responsibility and quite possibly the weather.

When I slowed to take a breath, Hadley said, "But Mom! You don't even know what's going on!"

I geared up to begin yet another lecture when I caught myself. She was right. I didn't know.

I wanted her ears to hear the correction I had for her when really, my ears needed to be the ones listening.

I was still right—she needed to watch her tone; but she was also right. I needed to tune in before turning on my voice.

Holy Spirit, thank You for my ability to listen. Place your hand over my mouth when I've said too much or spoken too soon. Keep my ears clear to hear those things which are most important in my life. And let me always be open to constructive criticism and correction, so I can become the person my Father in Heaven has created me to be. Amen and Amen.

-42-
Enter Mrs. Stuart

Moses' father-in-law said to him, "What you are doing isn't good. You will end up totally wearing yourself out, both you and these people who are with you. The work is too difficult for you. You can't do it alone."

Exodus 18:17-18

Hadley is passionate about history, government and social studies. When the opportunity to take AP European History arose, she didn't think twice about adding it to her schedule. She was confident the time and effort required by the course would meet her passion and interest in the subject area.

Then, the second week of school rolled around. The extreme pace of the course and the depth to which they were expected to know the subject left Hadley reeling. Her daddy is a social studies teacher, but his curricular area is geography. So, while he could help her with the basics of her content, it was no match for the teacher's expectations.

A friend of ours teaches American History in Hadley's building. I suggested she go speak to Lyndsey. Hadley, who could probably end up in

Lyndsey's her history class as well, was nervous at the prospect.

"I don't want her to think I'm dumb," she complained late one night. Hadley'd been up researching and reading and trying to come to her own conclusion as to what the teacher was looking for.

"I promise you," I assured her, "Mrs. Stuart will not think you are dumb."

A few more weeks went by with Hadley feeling utterly defeated by the class she was most looking forward to. She finally conceded. She needed help. She went to Mrs. Stuart.

Now, what I'm about to tell you will probably not serve as a surprise to 99.9% of you: Lyndsey Stuart, not only a friend of ours but a teacher in Hadley's discipline, was more than happy to help Hadley. Weird, huh? (Where's the sarcasm font when you need it?)

Since then, Hadley's discovered that she and Mrs. Stuart share political views, enjoy the same things, and even have a t-shirt in common. In fact, they wore their "Since 1920 #womensvotesmatter" t-shirts on the same day and Snapchatted it after they Instagrammed it.

Boom.

Mrs. Stuart not only gave Hadley some excellent resources to use and helped guide her in the proper direction, she served as a mentor to my kiddo ... and a friend to me.

So, why was it so hard for Hadley to ask for help?

Probably the same reason it's so hard for me to let go of the things I need to forgive.

Probably the same reason it's so hard for me to let Brian take over some of my responsibilities when I've just had enough.

Probably the same reason I push myself hard, stay up late, ignore my health, behave stubbornly, insist on the dishwasher being loaded my way, pout when the store rearranges their layout ... the list goes on.

We were never intended to walk through life alone. This is why there are many more people than just one. This is why God sent Jesus to bridge the gap between human and holy. This is why we reach out during the good times.

Let us, during all times—good and bad—seek out not only a person who can walk beside us, holding our hand and sharing our experience, but also seek out the One who created us to have relationships.

Generous Creator, for the gift of friendship and family, thank You. Forgive us when we foolishly believe we are more than enough for ourselves. Grant us wisdom to seek out those who can help us and, in all things, to seek out You as well. In the name of our bridge and our brother, Jesus, Amen.

-43-
Professionals

Let's behave appropriately as people who live in the day, not in partying and getting drunk, not in sleeping around and obscene behavior, not in fighting and obsession. Instead, dress yourself with the Lord Jesus Christ, and don't plan to indulge your selfish desires.
Romans 12:13-14

Without even watching one single minute of World Wide Wrestling Wacko-ness, my daughters have become experts at, well, faking it. Not that professional wrestling is fake, if that's what you believe ... riiiiiiiiiight.

My hubby and I suspected they were often times playing into the dramatic. But, so many of the "falls" and hits and kicks and curses came when an adult wasn't close enough to witness them, and we were hearing about it after the fact, typically, through crocodile tears or gritted teeth. Their reports of foul play were often times accompanied with pleas to "do something" and, when our something wasn't what they wanted, we were met with castigation as to our short-fallings as parents.

But, they each knew the tricks. Because our younger daughter is considerably stronger than her sister (and everyone else in the house), our older daughter often complained of physical pain that had been inflicted upon her by her baby sister.

And since the baby of the family was, well, the baby, her chief cry was that her sister used her words as swords, calling names and having her poor ears inflicted with curses that would make a sailor blush.

Up until a few years ago, my husband and I would successfully toss the problem solving back at our girls. "How are you going to solve this?" we'd ask, usually rhetorically. And the offended sister would pause, slink away and go make her peace with her sister.

Recently, however, their sibling squabbles have ratcheted up.

It was on a fateful Sunday morning when I confirmed our suspicions that their fights were as fake as a pro-wrestling match on a Saturday night at the fairgrounds.

We were preparing for church. I was ready way ahead of schedule and sat in the living room reading my devotional (fine, probably not ... I was probably scrolling through Facebook). My husband and mom were still getting ready in their respective rooms when the fighting began. It was kinda quiet and tame to begin with until my younger daughter came out and stood at the hall mirror, which was in my line of sight, after telling her sister that she had been in their bathroom first.

My older daughter then cried out, "Ouch! Don't touch me!"

My younger daughter responded, "Don't call me that!"

Their faux banter continued back and forth until my younger daughter finished applying her mascara. Her sister came out to the hallway and asked, "Where's Mom?"

As if they couldn't believe their badgering of one another hadn't drawn me to their sides to act as referee, they quieted their quarrelling and looked around. It was then that they saw me.

I didn't have to say a word. They dissolved into giggles at being caught fake fighting.

I'd like to tell you they learned their lesson and immediately stopped bickering. But, they didn't. They still fight as if their lives depended on it—and I'm still convinced that less than half of it is real.

I have noticed they aren't as quick to call out for a referee; they aren't as quick to continue a fight in front of us; and they are more honest in their complaints.

In this life, we're going to have battles; how we respond to them determines how people will see us.

Holy Father, we are so quick to abandon the high road for the sake of our own cause. We try to fool the people we are closest to, but we cannot fool You. When we are tempted to lead a deceitful life that is not glorifying to You, call to us and remind us that You've given us a beautiful life with Jesus. In Your stillness we stand and pray. Amen.

-44-

Who Cares What They Think

You must be holy in every aspect of your lives,
just as the one who called you is holy.
I Peter 1:15

One advantage to having your kids attend the same school in which you teach is that you will ultimately get to know all of their classmates. Since my husband and I both teach on different seventh grade teams; if I didn't have a kid in class on my academic teaching team, my husband would have that kid through his team. Therefore, our kiddos must choose their friends wisely.

With that being said, we have absolutely no complaints with any of their friends at all. These friends aren't perfect, but they are pretty close.

As I pulled out the couch one day to sweep behind it (crazy how those empty chip bags belonging to no one find their ways back there), I discovered a note to Hadley from an acquaintance of hers.

Initially, I laughed because who writes a note these days when everyone has a device or two or three on which a simple text can be sent. I started to not even read it, but if it had been personal, surely she wouldn't have stashed it in an old crumpled up

Cheeto bag, right? Plus, this could be my girl's first and only note!

A few years prior, she and the note giver had been closer friends, but as often happens, time and friendships march on. His school path had taken him down a different road than Hadley's, due in part to their varied interest, they no longer considered themselves friends—Hadley's term was "friendly but not friends" when I asked her about him.

The note was short and to the point, much like the writer himself. It said, in no uncertain terms, that he didn't appreciate her language. "Knock it off on the swearing" were his exact words.

I carried the note to her and asked what he meant and why he'd written a note about it.

"Well," she said, "he keeps saying he's moving, and so he wrote us all notes telling us how we could fix ourselves and make ourselves better." This sounded very much like him. "I guess he thinks I should cuss less," she continued very matter of factly.

"Do you think you should cuss less?" I questioned her, knowing the answer should be a resounding yes because she, like me, had a propensity for four-letter words.

"Maybe," she conceded, "but why should I care what he thinks?"

This is a fine line for girls to walk. I don't want her to alter her behavior just because some boy says she should, but I also don't want her to become known as the school's potty mouth, if she's not already.

I took a deep breath, probably alternating between a prayer and a swear, and gave her my best answer.

She shouldn't care what he thinks. He's her "friendly non-friend," or whatever, so he shouldn't dictate how she lives her life. But ...

She should care what the God who created her and gave her the life she's living thinks. She should be aware that when she takes on the nametag of "Follower" she'll be inviting others to judge her faith and her God based on her behavior.

"So," I sighed, "don't be more aware of your language because your non-friend has told you to, but do it because you want to be the best reflection of God at all times."

She nodded her head and said, "I gotcha." I think she means that she'll try her best.

It's not easy to communicate with teenagers. It's not easy to communicate when you are a teenager. It's not easy to stop yourself when a cuss word is so handy during certain situations, like a stubbed toe or a dropped drink.

But, it can be easy to be a reflection of the Holy One.

Holy and understanding God, You have called us to follow You in being Holy in all parts of our lives, including our language. Let us not be tempted to behave as the world would have us to behave, but to act and respond so that we reflect the love and grace that comes only from You. In the name of our savior we pray, Amen.

-45-
First Day Survival Techniques

Be strong! Be fearless! Don't be afraid
and don't be scared by your enemies,
because the Lord your God
is the one who marches with you.
He won't let you down, and he won't abandon you.
Deuteronomy 31:6

I was fortunate enough to get to be library-media specialist at the elementary school where we sent our daughters. At the end of Hadley's fourth grade year, though, the school board decided to close our school.

I would be moved to the middle school downtown, and we'd put Hadley and Briley in the elementary school just a few blocks away. Initially, this would be the school their besties attended as well. Before school started, the plan was for them to walk from my building to their elementary together.

Then, toward the end of the summer, their besties moved to south Texas, leaving my girls to make the walk alone.

We practiced the path they would walk; we secured them with basic cell phones "just in case"; and we tried to find as many people as we could who would be attending the same school—there weren't that many.

The night before school started, we walked from my building to their building with their school supplies bundled on their backs for "Meet The

Teacher" night. After placing their items in their new desks in their new rooms in their new school, we walked back toward my building with the sun beginning to set.

And that's when it hit me: This would be the first first day of school I'd have missed with my girls. I have never been a helicopter mom, so it was a new feeling for me. Or maybe I was a helicopter mom, but had never had to hover since we'd always been in the same building. Or maybe I could just pull them out of elementary school and enroll them in middle school and still have them with me all the time. Sure it sounds ridiculous now that I've typed it, but believe me when I say at that time, it was a completely sane and viable option.

The world, after all—especially elementary school, is a scary place.

But, I kept myself in check. I reigned in my emotions as I tended to the girls and their own very real frets and worries of *what if I forget my lunch?* And *what if a stray dog chases us?* And *what if the stray dog turns out to be friendly and homeless and is waiting for us when school lets out and follows us back to your building and jumps in the minivan and goes home with us?*

The first day of school arrived, and we were all up extra early. We were all dressed and had our empty backpacks secure on our backs. We had our lunches packed and a plan in place for stray dogs. (Hint: They all had homes to go back to.)

The first bell at my school was the signal for my daughters to begin their walk. With a kiss and a prayer, I sent them to their new school. They were giddy (probably at the prospect of finding that one homeless dog). I was not so much.

From the moment we have our children placed into our arms, we begin to teach them independence, eating on their own, moving by themselves, sleeping through the night. And, it never does get easier to see them take the next big leap to becoming a productive citizen of this world.

In fact, it's scary: Not all of the dogs, literally and figuratively, in our world are friendly.

But, we have God who walks with us. He stays with us. He guides us and, even though He knows we are afraid, He has made us to be strong. It's not easy, for sure, to let our kids go. It is, however, comforting to know that God is beside us as we see them skip down the street toward their next adventure.

Heavenly Father, sometimes this life is full of tough situations that leave us feeling weak. Slip Your arms around our shoulders, encouraging us to lean into You as we let open our hands and send our children into the world. In the name of Your Son, who came into this world to save us, Amen.

-46-

Being Forced Isn't Always That Bad

By Hadley

For everyone who asks, receives.
Whoever seeks, finds.
And to everyone who knocks, the door is opened.
Matthew 7:8

When I was in eighth grade, I was searching. I was searching for somewhere I belonged. I was done with sports, there was way too much running and definitely too much sweat, even though golf was my favorite sport, which doesn't always involve running or sweating, I just didn't feel like my heart was in it enough to compete for my team.

My dad told me I had to do an extra-curricular, and he thought I would like Science Olympiad, an after school organization run by a fellow teacher. I fought him tooth and nail not to go; I was content with what I was currently doing, which was basically reading books in my room and staying current on the new YouTube videos. He finally told me I had to go to "just three meetings", and if I didn't like it, I didn't have to go back.

WELL, OKAY, DAD!

Not thrilled with my mandate, I walked into that first "practice" and immediately thought *Wow, this lady's desk is messy*. But, she walked in and was nothing but a bundle of energy, fluttering from kid to kid answering questions and making suggestions, directing experiments. I was amazed at what we had already accomplished and how quickly I was swept into several Science Olympiad events after only a brief conversation.

Long story short: I went to three meetings, then four meetings, then five. That lady had me hooked.

Her name was Mrs. Herron. She taught seventh grade science. I didn't have her as a teacher. I had another teacher and, maybe, because I was a seventh grader or maybe because of circumstances I'm not fully aware of, my teacher lacked Mrs. Herron's passion and drive. I had pretty much written off science as something I wasn't interested in.

Until Mrs. Herron.

She guided me and aided me in winning six medals that year at state competitions, and guided our group as a whole into placing third in the state two years in a row. Because of her and her alone, I've gone from being a fluttery middle school student to a sophomore, a potential future scientist and engineer.

I have now had three years to observe her like a true scientist and my conclusion is this: She is the most kind, honest, sincere teacher I have ever met. I'm grateful I "stuck it out" for those three meetings because she's helped and is helping me to chart the course of the rest of my life, and she is most deserving of this honor.

Sometimes parents do know what they are talking about. And not all adults are stuffy and huffy.

For the adults You place in my life, Father, thank You. You know just what we need and who we need and know how to get it to us; we just have to listen to You. When we are seeking, remind us You will help us find what we need. In the name of Jesus I pray, Amen.

-47-

Winning and Losing

Am I trying to win over human beings or God?
Or am I trying to please people?
If I were still trying to please people,
I won't be Christ's slave.
Galatians 1:10

I have won a creative writing contest in our hometown several years in a row. The contest has several categories in which to enter. Even though I'd won accolades and awards for my humor writing, which is non-fiction, I'd never won a non-fiction category in this particular contest. Go figure. For whatever reason, I just couldn't write to please those non-fiction judges.

The contest is also open to students, judged separately from the adults, of course. Once a student is 14 years old, she may enter for free. Cash is the award, so it's a no-brainer, at least to me, that Hadley, my little budding writer, entered as soon as she turned 14.

That year, she won. We went to the award ceremony where she and two of her friends swept the student division, claiming all the prizes and loading up on big, fat checks. Well, as big and fat as you can get in a medium-sized city's local contest.

I didn't win. I thought of the editors I'd worked with. The publishers who'd hired me and actually did pay me. I thought of how I was confident in my own writing, but I still just couldn't crack what the judges wanted.

The next year, Hadley and I worked hard on our entries. I studied who had won in year's past and just knew this was the year I was going to crack that contest right open and come home with a big prize in my chosen area.

Hadley submitted a couple of poems and a few short stories. She was even interviewed for the newspaper as a previous winner and spoke gracefully about why she enjoys writing and why she enjoys the contest.

The week came when winners were notified so they could attend the award's ceremony. They didn't know what they'd won; only that they had won.

A fellow classmate of Hadley's posted on social media that she'd received an email announcing she'd won.

I checked my email, nothing.

I checked Hadley's email (don't tell her), nothing.

I texted her and asked her to check it. Maybe she had a super secret inbox that I wasn't aware of. She had nothing.

Then I justified that perhaps they'd only told one person and then got distracted. The internet is full of shiny diversions. We'd wait a day. Or Two. Maybe one more.

By the end of the week, neither of us had been notified of winning. My heart sunk not only for me, but for my kiddo as well.

"Hadley," I very gingerly and sweetly called as I entered her bedroom. "I'm sorry you didn't win. Maybe you can get a copy of the winning entries from your friends so you'll know what the judges are looking for."

"Why?" she asked.

"Because," I explained slowly, "if you know what the judges are looking for, you can write specifically for them and win next year."

She shrugged. "But I really write for me not the judges."

I sighed.

My kid is so smart.

I shouldn't change who I am or what I do to please a creative writing judge. The only concern I should have should be to please my Creator, who gave me my talents.

Sometimes I am so silly, Father. I get so caught up in beating a system to get man-given recognition, I'm sure I've distorted my God-given talents. Don't let my whims take me from the place where I use my talents for You. And, never cease to place a teacher in my path to help me learn lessons I'm slow to take in—even if that teacher is my daughter. In the name of Jesus my Savior, Amen.

-48-
Don't Wake Me Before Noon

Come to me, all you who are struggling hard and carrying heavy loads, and I will give you rest.
Matthew 11:28

One of my greatest pleasures in life since I can ever remember is sleeping late. I like to sleep without an alarm and until my body tells me it's time to get up. If this ever does happen (it rarely does), I can sleep until well after ten in the morning.

Guess what? Having kids did nothing to allow me to continue experiencing this preference of mine. Those little boogers liked waking up early—well *before* ten.

Hadley used to be such an early riser, that we had to retrain her to wake up. She'd naturally wake up around 5:30. Then when the time changed, She naturally woke up at 4:30. Y'all? Prior to kids, I thought that 4:30 in the a.m. was just an urban legend. So, Brian and I would get up at 4:15 to wake her up. Then, after a week or so, when we felt like she was getting used to our waking her up, we'd wake her up about 4:45, then 5:00, then 5:30, then 6:30. That's when Brian would take her and do the breakfast stuff, and I would get to rest a little bit longer.

Friends, I was blessed among mommas.

Fast forward fifteen years. Many night, Hadley's still completing a Spanish translation or a response from European History or annotating a text of world literature well into the morning hours.

Then, she has to wake up to go to school early in the morning ... because unfortunately, that's when school starts.

So, on the weekends that she's not working or doesn't have any other plans, she sleeps in. Her preferred waking time this past weekend was two in the afternoon.

This works well for me because it means I get to sleep in to a certain extent. But, after I'm awake and going strong, I start itching to wake her. I am reminded of the time we had to teach her to sleep in and how she used to shuck naps and how sleeping was something she used to not be interested in.

And now, I'm convinced, if the house caught fire around noon on a Saturday, she'd lay in bed and try to blow the fire out while still half-dozing.

But, I know she's doing it right.

This world has become more busy than it's ever been before. When I was Hadley's age, if I needed something from the discount store for school, I'd better have it before nine o'clock in the p. m.. After nine o'clock, all the stores were closed. Now, if Hadley needs something at three in the morning (which has happened, y'all), we have our choice of a multitude of 24-hour super stores that are ready and willing to sell us whatever we need.

If we want the answer to any question, it's only a click away on the world wide web. If we want to talk to a friend, we can call or Skype or Facetime without time delay.

We aren't getting the rest we need. The world commands and allows us to stay awake and be as active as we want.

But, just as He commanded His disciples, Jesus commands us: Break away, rest. Steal away from the world. And if that rest comes in the form of sleeping in on weekends, so be it. It's what Jesus tells us to do.

Jesus, the giver of all things, thank You for the gift of rest. Thank You for recognizing we cannot do all things and cannot be a part of this world at all times. We need our breaks. Help us create the space and the place we need to take our rest from the world so we can be renewed and refreshed for the greater ministries You call us to. In You name we pray. Amen.

-49-
Really Good Acoustics

He put a new song in my mouth,
a song of praise for our God.
Many people will learn of this and be amazed;
they will trust the Lord.
Psalm 40:3

Imma start this off with a very tired (yet still very true) cliché: Kids these days don't know how good they have it. I know! I'm just one waving fist away from screaming at kids to get off my lawn!

When I was their age (here I go again), I had to save up my baby sitting money to buy 45 rpm records of hit songs (mainly because I wasn't patient enough to save up enough money to buy a full LP). Then, I had to be extra careful to not scratch it on my record player.

Eventually, I graduated up to recording the songs from the radio to a cassette tape (pretty sure we broke all kinds of copyright laws with our pre-Napster way of getting songs for free). It was a crying shame when the DJ talked right up to the point when Cyndi Lauper began singing.

These days, my girls just save up their money to buy an iTunes card (or convince me that I, myself, like the song) and then download it, easy-breezy beautiful. And what's more: They take their devices into the bathroom with their blue-tooth speakers to have a glorious in-shower concert at their disposal.

I sound all crotchety and old, but, in fact, I kinda enjoy their shower time singing. If they're taking their shower late at night, which is almost always, Brian and I get to lay in bed and listen to them. Their tastes range from some modern stuff like Taylor Swift or the latest boy band to the good stuff like Queen and the Beatles. It's eclectic as well. Some playlists include songs like "Oceans" right after the theme song to *Rent*, which comes right before the amazing sounds of JOHNNYSWIM. Eclectic, y'all.

And because they are teenage girls, their showers can last almost as long as a Twenty-one Pilots concert.

Because I'm their momma, I can say with a confidence that exceeds all understanding, my daughters have incredibly beautiful voices. On occasion, Briley let's her voice take on the tone of an *American Idol* contestant, but for the most part, they both sound lovely.

Neither one, however, is in choir. Hadley gave orchestra a go and sang in children's choir in church. Briley was in school choir for a year, but found it was "so much more than an episode of *American Idol*" and opted to take Spanish instead.

But still, they sing in the shower.

After one particularly long shower which culminated in a beautiful rendition of Leonard Cohen's "Hallelujah" (is there any other kind of rendition of that song?), I asked Hadley—nay, I begged her—to join a choir, any choir, let her sweet voice be heard by those of us who do not reside within earshot of the shower.

"Nah," she blew me off, "I'm good."

"I know!" I countered. "You are good! You need to be in a choir!"

"Nope. That's not for me," she answered with certainty before retreating to her room, where she probably Snapchatted about her mom standing outside the bathroom door during her showers.

She will probably never join a choir, but I do hear her sing during church and as long as she lives at home and practices good hygiene, I'll get to hear her sing in the shower. But, I'll count it as a dadgum shame that no one else will get to hear her.

The thought makes me wonder: Are there times when I fail to sing the praises of my God, my Savior, my Heavenly Father? Don't answer that. I know the answer. There are many times when the things He has done for me and provided for me fill me with a song that I fail to sing. What a dadgum shame that others might not know of His goodness because I refuse to sing outside of my own comfort zone. Hadley's nervous about singing for others. I hope, however, she (and I and you and all of us) can learn to sing His praises so that others can know our God is King.

Generous God, who never fails to give us good things, forgive us when the song in our heart goes unsung. Forgive us when we fail to praise You and acknowledge the goodness that comes from You. And forgive us when we miss an opportunity to share Your grace with our neighbors. In the name of the one who sings the sweetest song of all, Amen.

-50-
Even In The Minivan

Jesus said to her, "Believe me, woman, the time is coming when you and your people will worship the Father neither on this mountain nor in Jerusalem."
John 4:21

Our niece, Naomi, was born in December. (All of our nieces, along with my own kids were born around the holidays, except for one—she was born at the beginning of the school year, kinda the same busy-ness!) Because it's a busy time of year, my sister-in-law tried to be accommodating in planning Naomi's birthday party. So, a Sunday afternoon in early December, we set out on a four-hour journey to eat cake and ice cream.

True to form of sisters who were having to endure each other on a quick day trip, Hadley and Briley started our journey with an argument. We weren't even off of our block before we had put our teenage daughters on a tongue time out to keep them from speaking.

When their silence was paroled, I asked them to tell me their favorite worship song. We were missing church, after all, and thanks to technology, a little iTunes and an aux cord, we could have church right there in the minivan on our way to southern Oklahoma.

"Oceans, I guess," one of them answered, opting for the easy way out (because, let's face it, who doesn't love "Oceans"?)

"Great Are You Lord," came another answer.

I scrolled through my songs and tapped them into a playlist as they continued to name songs.

"Blessed Be Your Name"

"Came To My Rescue"

"Build Your Kingdom Here"

Eventually, I just hit shuffle and let the music play.

For an hour and a half, we cruised down the highway, singing our hearts out and enjoying the music we were missing since we were missing church.

I'm not claiming that on any given morning worship songs soothe the savage beasts. There have been plenty of rides that I've thrown on some Hillsong or All Sons and Daughters only to have to turn it off before the first verse ends and scream a threat that involves kicking both children onto the side of the road as if they were dirty Samarians.

But on that particular morning, we worshiped in the minivan driving down a highway on our way to a birthday party.

In John, Jesus travels through Samaria. He meets a Samarian woman at the well. He asks her for a drink. She obliges, but not without questions.

Why do you want my water?

Where is the living well?

Where should we worship?

And he replies that the time is coming where, she and all of us, can worship wherever we find the spirit and wherever we find the truth.

We live in a time where we know the savior. We live in a place where we can worship where and how we are moved. We live as children of God and that's an empowering thought.

Even in a minivan.

Thank You, Father, for adopting us into Your family and enabling us to worship as the spirit leads us. Keep us mindful, there are those who don't know how or are not able to worship You. Draw us to them so that, like Jesus, we can tell them of the living water You will cleanse us with. In the name of our open and welcoming savior, Amen and Amen.

-51-
A Mom By Any Other Name

A child is born to us, a song is given to us,
And authority will be on his shoulders.
He will be named
Wonderful Counselor, Mighty God,
Eternal Father, Prince of Peace.
Isaiah 9:6

One of the first "tricks" we taught Hadley as a toddler was to say *excuse me* when she wanted our attention. When she interrupted us, the others we were talking to found such delight and amusement in her interruption. Often, they'd remark that they thought she was precious.

The next trick we attempted to teach her was patience. Just because she said *excuse me* didn't mean we had to stop our conversation and tend to her every whim. The resulting fit was very rarely precious.

To this end, Hadley quickly learned I might not always answer to momma. If I knew her need was not immediately important, I'd often times say, "Not now," and return my attention to whomever I was speaking to. This would usually end in Hadley calling me as many names as she knew for me.

"Momma! Momma!"

"Mooooom!"

"Mommy!"

"Maaaaaaaaaaaaaaaaaaaaaaamaaaaaaaaaaaaa!"

If I was doing a good job of ignoring her, thinking I was teaching her a lesson, she'd often times resort to calling me *Heather*. And, if she'd recently been around a student of mine, she'd call me *Mrs. Davis*.

If she were really and truly annoyed with me, she'd call me *Lady*.

As in, "Hey, Lady! Let me go over there!" while in the middle of Hellmart, walking past the toy section.

Once, as I was making her stand in line with me at the photo processing center (when people still developed pictures), she hollered out a "Let go of me, *Lady*" after a Code Adam announcement for a missing child. (It was soon-after cancelled. See what happens when you let go of them?!)

Now that she's a teenager, Hadley still has many names for me. Her sweet *Momma* has shortened to *Mom*. When she's annoyed, it's *Mother*, usually through gritted teeth. When we're at a school function, it's *Heather*, knowing that most kids call me Mrs. Davis or occasionally slip up and call me Mom. The *Lady* has dropped from her vernacular, maybe because she's way too big for me to hang on to her. And, late at night, when she's sick or had a bad dream, she cries out *Maaaaaaamaaaaaa*.

In much the same way, we cry out to our Creator using different names: A counselor who guides us; a God who creates us; a Father who parents us; a Prince who rules us.

His names are many—Alpha, Omega, I Am, Jesus, Messiah, Lord, Christ.

And we can rest assured that when we call out to Him, regardless of how or what we cry, He hears us.

Holy God who is known by many names, thank You that when You hear our voice, You open Your ears to hear us. You listen when we call, whether we call You in praise, in worship, in hurt, in sadness, in gladness, in the morning or in the night. Your name is high above all else, and Your ability to hear our voice among all the other noises in heaven and earth is greater than we will ever know. Praying through Christ, our brother, our lord and our friend, Amen.

-52-

Deep Under The Sand

Ever since the creation of the world, God's
invisible qualities
—God's eternal power and divine nature—
have been clearly seen,
because they are understood
through the things God has made.
So humans are without excuse.
Romans 1:20

We decided to spend Thanksgiving week at the beach. Five years before, our best friends had moved to south Texas and we'd only seen them once since. They lived a block from the beach and welcomed us with open arms.

When we first arrived at the beach, Hadley walked toward the water's edge. A group of mussels were unearthed by the waves. She squatted down to watch them shimmy just under the sand before the next wave barreled over them, uncovering them yet again. Without any prompting, and forgetting her sister and friends were getting their wetsuits on and grabbing surf boards, she sat down beside the mussel group and watched for a good while as they burrowed themselves in vain, only to be exposed with the next lap of the Gulf's waters.

Finally, she walked back to where we sat, watching the other girls surf, or attempt to surf as the case may be. As she squirreled on her wetsuit, she marveled at the mussels.

"I've never seen anything like that!" she squealed. "There should be absolutely no reason for them to move, no reason for them to know they've been uncovered, no reason for them to know which way to shimmy themselves under the sand, but they do, time and again. It's pretty amazing!"

I grinned at her. It was rare that anything amazed our fifteen-year-old smarty-pants.

We spent a full day at the beach and returned home tired and fulfilled, Hadley was still marveling at the mussels, even though she hadn't found a group of them again.

The next day, we headed back to the beach, checking out a different area, though. Our hosts promised us that this would be more local and we'd see more people surfing, kite-boarding, fishing. Plus, the waves would be better since Briley was still trying to get up and stay up on her board.

We parked the cars and Hadley dashed to the water's edge again. She kicked once at the sand. Then again. Then retreated back to the vehicles.

"There are no mussels," she announced with a faux disappointment, even though I knew there was a slight bit of authentic disappointment outlining her face.

"Oh, they are there," her daddy assured her. "We just can't see them."

"Well," Hadley sighed with a grin. "I wanted to see them."

Oh sweet girl of mine. We all want to see them. We want to see the fascinating and marvelous and amazing things. But, that's what makes our faith strong.

When the things of the world—the wrecking waves of disappointment, the dirty sand of relationships, the heft of the obligations that our lives heap upon us—when those things bury the fascinating and wonderful nature of our Heavenly Father, we have to believe that He's still there.

If she'd have the gumption to dig deep enough, she'd have found mussels.

If we have the desire and drive to dig through the mess that this world throws onto us, we'd find God.

In all times. In all places. In all ways. God is ever-present. Don't be disappointed when you cannot find Him. Dig through the sand, withstand the waves, He's waiting on you.

Heavenly Father, creator of all things divine and delightful, forgive us when we fail to look for You. When the world beats us down, call to us and give us the strength to look for You. Remind us that finding You in the weariness of our lives is a welcome reminder that You are always close. In the precious name of Jesus, we pray. Amen.

Acknowledgements

I love all of God's ideas (some of them take some time…). But I especially love the idea that he gave to me with this series of devotionals. Thanks for trusting and energizing me, Good, Good Father.

I'm grateful that God trusted me enough (probably too much) to give me such amazing daughters. I always wanted sons. I feared the teenage years. But God's plans are better than my plans, and I got Hadley and Briley. I'm so grateful that I could share in writing this book with Hadley. She's the one on the cover, FYI. Isn't she beautiful!?

My girls have never known a time that I haven't written about them. They've stopped running away from home and just hibernate in their rooms. Most of the time, though, they are willing subjects. They make my job easy. Notice I didn't say they made my life easy …

My hubby has stayed up countless hours with me while I was writing. And by stayed up, I mean he slept in the recliner, but it's the thought that counts. I know for a fact I couldn't see my dreams as a writer come true without him. I'm beyond thankful I get to do life with him.

My mom was very instrumental in my getting this book written. The times when I needed inspiration, she'd come along and play a Facebook video on her iPad that was so distracting I had no choice but to toss in my earbuds and get a little praise party happening in my head.

Marilyn Boone, Christine Jarmola, Jennifer McMurrain and Cindy Molder have been reading my words for many years now. Their insight is invaluable, and I couldn't imagine writing a book without their eyes and thoughts. Thank you, friends! I'll cheer for your anatomy anytime. (Also, check out their books—they're great!)

A gazillion thank yous and eleventy-million I love yous to Alyssa Foresman who rallies beside me at every turn of this crazy life. She's a great go-to gal. I hope every one of you gets to have an Alyssa in your life.

Thanks to Emily Call and Harriot Gilbertson for sharing their lives and the lives of their daughters with me and my girls. Not a day goes by that I'm not filled with thankfulness for their friendships.

I'm thrilled to be working with fellow girl-mom, Lisa Kuehn of Dream On Marketing & Consulting, on this project. She designed the cover and made me look all kinds of snazzy. She also has a boy, a farm, livestock, her own business and doesn't judge me harshly when she doesn't hear from me for a month (or three). She knows. Y'all? She knows.

And finally, I'm grateful for you, lovely readers. If it weren't for you, this would just be a lonely little book, sitting on a bookshelf. Thanks for reading and praying with me.

About Heather Davis

I am a momma, a writer, a blogger, a humorist, and I have a finely tuned ability to share every last detail of my life with anyone who will read or listen. My first book, TMI Mom Oversharing My Life, is a number 1 best seller, and it has led the way for three more TMI Mom books: Getting Lucky, Crazy on Board and Girlfriend Rules. My fifth book Life With Extra Cheese, was released with rave reviews. When I'm not jetting off to NYC to appear on national talk shows (okay–it's only been one show), I live in Bartlesville with my very patient husband, Brian, and our two crazy daughters. The nuts don't fall far from the tree.

About Hadley Davis

Hadley is the first-born daughter of Heather & Brian. She tricked them into thinking that being parents was easy by being the world's best baby. Then she became one, began speaking in complete dissertations, crawled out of her crib and pronounced that she didn't "yike yucky peas." Despite her parents' best successes and failures, she has survived through her sophomore year in high school and plans to "maybe go to college" and "maybe pick a major." She loves her sister despite what her actions (and sometimes her words) indicate, and her parents know she's going to change the world. If she had come out of her room, she might have written a better biography for herself.

Other Books By Heather Davis

Oversharing My Life
Getting Lucky
Crazy On Board
Girlfriend Rules
Life With Extra Cheese
Sundays At The Fields

Available in eBook only

We're Not The Cleavers
Still Not The Cleavers
What The Elf Saw

From Life With Extra Cheese

I like to imagine that the ER nurse pulled Dr. Jim Bob to the side and said, "Dude!" as she slapped him upside the head, knocking some sense into him saying they were going to send this incontinent, unable to stand, drawn-faced woman home. The next time he came into the room, he said they were planning on admitting her, and she could see the neurologist on Monday. She'd been in the hospital for over six hours at this point.

I was almost forty-four. My sister was almost forty. But, when I looked at her sitting beside me in that curtain-walled room, I saw a much younger version of my sister.

She was three years old when our dad had his first heart attack. I was seven. Two years later, he had another heart attack and then faced open-heart surgery. I remember sitting at the dinner table one night before we went to Tulsa for the big surgery, and my daddy telling us that he never wanted to be kept alive by machines.

In my little kid mind, I imagined that some robot, looking much like R2D2 from Star Wars, continuing to perform CPR on my dad so he wouldn't die.

When my dad had his first stroke almost ten years after his first heart attack, he said the same thing, "I don't want any damn machines keeping me alive."

He also told us that he didn't want us to have a funeral for him because they were too expensive. He wanted to be cremated and then tossed to the side.

At the age of sixteen, I knew my dad's exact plans for his end-of-life. And with each health event that we paced through with my dad, my sister looked exactly the same. She looked like the three year old, tow-headed scared little girl. Regardless of how old she really was.

At the age of sixty-nine, my dad had his final heart attack and final stroke. Having no brain activity at all, we removed him from the life support machines—which looked nothing like R2D2—and three days later, he died. My sister was almost twenty-eight at the time. She looked like she was three.

My mom's plans were very different, though.

They were very different because we never talked about them. I had some ideas, though. I wanted my mom to die when she was ninety-nine years old, peacefully in her sleep in her own home having gone to bed the night before with a sound mind. I wanted her to have her hands crossed on her chest and fresh daisies beside her bed. I wanted the neighborhood birds to be perched above her bedroom window whistling "It Is Well With My Soul."

I wanted my mom to die in a Disney movie, apparently. My way still beats being trampled by wildebeests for sure.

~~~

As I sat in the emergency room wondering why they didn't just catheterize my mom's bladder already, I realized that all of my plans were changing.

My younger daughter, who had just turned ten, had just joined a competitive softball team. Her schedule was slam-packed with practices, travel and tournaments. My older daughter, who was twelve, was on the middle school golf team and played cello in the orchestra. Not that there's any good time for a stroke to happen, but now was really *not* a good time as far as I was concerned. I didn't ask my mom, but I'm sure she would have agreed.

We didn't have to take my mom to our house that day. She was admitted. I didn't have to go all Macgyver and catheterize her myself with a drinking straw, brightly-patterned duct tape and a Ziploc baggie. I didn't go home that night. I didn't sleep that night.

I did eat a McGaggle's cheeseburger at about nine o'clock that night. My mom looked over at me from her hospital bed and said, "You know that's how this all started."
~~~

32677910R00096

Made in the USA
Lexington, KY
05 March 2019